EMPOWERMENT
E T H I C S
FOR A LIBERATED PEOPLE

Please return to

Stephen Carlyle

509-781-2201

EMPOWERMENT
E T H I C S
FOR A LIBERATED PEOPLE

A Path to
African American
Social Transformation

Cheryl J. Sanders

Fortress Press
Minneapolis

EMPOWERMENT ETHICS FOR A LIBERATED PEOPLE
A Path to African American Social Transformation

Biblical quotations unless otherwise noted are from the New Revised Standard Version Bible, copyright © by the Division of Christian Education of the National Council of the Churches of Christ in the United States of America. Used by permission.

Chapter 5, "Achievement," appeared in a different version as "Ethics and the Educational Achievements of Black Women," in *Religion and Intellectual Life* 5, no. 4 (Summer 1988).

Cover graphic: John T. Biggers, *Shotguns,* oil and acrylic on canvas, 1987. 40 × 56 inches. Private collection. Used by permission of the artist. Photograph courtesy of the Dallas Museum of Art (see p. 141).
Cover design: Lois Stanfield, LightSource Images
Author photo: George Abiad

Library of Congress Cataloging-in-Publication Data

Sanders, Cheryl Jeanne.
    Empowerment ethics for a liberated people : a path to African
American social transformation / Cheryl J. Sanders.
        p.   cm.
    Includes bibliographical references and index.
    ISBN 0-8006-2917-5 (alk. paper)
    1. Afro-Americans—Religion.   2. Liberation theology.
3. Christian ethics.   4. Social ethics.   5. United States—Church
history—20th century.   6. United States—Race relations.
I. Title.
BR563.N4S36   1995
277.3′08′08996073—dc20   95-24836
                                                                    CIP

The paper used in this publication meets the minimum requirements of American National Standard for Information Sciences—Permanence of Paper for Printed Library Materials, ANSI Z329.4-1984.

Manufactured in the U.S.A.   AF 1-2917

                    4   5   6   7   8   9   10

For Allison and Garrett

Contents

Handwritten margin note (left side, vertical): Each of these approaches represents a model of ① focused moral reflection and ② Social Action

vii

Contents

Preface

This book describes how Christian spirituality and ethics have shaped African American notions of moral progress from the nineteenth century to the present. It also examines how religious commitment relates to social responsibility in the life and work of African American Christians. The term *empowerment ethics* refers to the norms, values, and principles that have guided this people's journey from slavery to liberation and from victimization to moral agency. Empowerment ethics is lifted up here as a theme for the continued progress of a people "in charge"—those who have acquired access to the goods and services of the society and who are challenged to direct their own institutions and administer their own resources in ways that are liberating and empowering for those who still languish in poverty and despair. The analysis of African American moral progress is grounded in a paradigm of seven approaches to empowerment— testimony, protest, uplift, cooperation, achievement, remoralization, and ministry—each of which represents a mode of focused moral reflection and social action on the part of conscientious Christians in response to the plight and prospects of an oppressed African American people.

Preface

My acknowledgments begin with a word of thanks to Dr. Preston N. Williams, Houghton Professor of Theology and Contemporary Change at Harvard Divinity School, who has been my mentor and colleague in the study of Christian ethics and African American religion. I must also thank the deans, faculty, and staff of the Howard University School of Divinity for their continued support and encouragement. I owe a special debt to my Howard students, among them pastors, bishops, teachers, lawyers, social workers, military officers, government officials, corporate executives, and other "empowered" professionals whose questions, essays, and papers have kept me attuned to the basic concerns addressed in this book.

My church family at the Third Street Church of God has produced a steady stream of credible role models for Christian spirituality, ethics, and ministry.

Finally, I am forever grateful for the love and patience of my family. I was born into the Sanders family; my mother, Doris, my father, Wallace, and my brother, Eric, have all been there for me from the beginning. My husband, Alan Carswell, has been constant in his loving commitment to our marriage and family life. And our two children, Allison Joy and Garrett Jeremiah, to whom this book is dedicated, have embodied for me, day by day, the truthfulness and struggle that empower my people.

INTRODUCTION
Ethics for a People "In Charge"

The paradigm of African American moral thought since 1969 has been black liberation theology, whose approach has emphasized a critique of oppression, affirmation of the humanity of the oppressed, and evaluation of the experience of the oppressed as a source and criterion for truth. This paradigm is foundational in the work of a growing number of theologians and ethicists influenced by James H. Cone, the seminal thinker in this regard.[1] Black liberation theology is an invaluable starting point for discussion of the past plight and future prospects of the African American people. A further step begs to be explored in the present-day moral reflections of African American Christians, however, based on a critical question left largely unanswered by black liberation theologians and ethicists. What sources of ethical guidance are available for those individuals and groups who have made the transition from victimization to moral agency, that is, for those who are already experiencing liberation? What light can liberation theology and ethics shed upon the moral challenges faced by African American men and women who are in charge of their own institutions and resources, given that the liberatory discourse has primarily been pursued by and among persons who are comfortably ensconced within the elite academic structures of the dominant culture. How can such persons be encouraged to retain a strong sense of identity and level of engagement with those who have not yet experienced liberation?

Some answers to this question are set forth in this book under the rubric "empowerment ethics for a liberated people." The ethics of liberation grounded in the dialectics of oppressor versus oppressed needs to be modified to provide more suitable norms for moral decision making by those who have moved beyond liberation and protest to assume positions of spiritual and material empowerment. The black liberation theologian's moral critique of the oppressing group is a necessary but insufficient condition for fostering African American moral progress. What is also warranted is the constructive ethical task of delineating steps to be taken by the oppressed to ensure that the experience of empowerment does not result in assimilation of the most dehumanizing values and behaviors of the oppressing group, and in reduplication of intragroup oppression. Indeed, meaningful moral progress toward justice can be derived neither from the internalization of the oppressor's values nor from the insistence that one's own liberation is always someone else's obligation.

In their landmark 1990 study of black churches, C. Eric Lincoln and Lawrence H. Mamiya found that since black liberation theology is a relatively recent intellectual movement occurring largely among the educated elite of the black clergy, it has had a limited impact upon the black churches; "the great majority of black urban ministers in the United States—at least two-thirds of them—have not been affected by the movement at all."[2] Notwithstanding the practical limitations of black theological discourse, in general the Christian faith offers a clear rationale for establishing ministering relationships across the lines of sex, race, and class. Christians of all races can be found doing the work of ministry, propelled to enact, and not merely to quote, the foundational Gospel text for prophetic engagement in the name of Christ, Luke 4:18:

Jesus Quotes Isaiah₂

Ethics for a People "In Charge"

> The Spirit of the Lord is upon me,
> because he has anointed me
> to bring good news to the poor.
> He has sent me to proclaim release to the captives
> and recovery of sight to the blind,
> to let the oppressed go free.

Pharisees -
The Oppressers
as well as the oppressed

An expanded understanding of discipleship also motivates conscientious Christians to embrace Matthew 25:40, which requires service of Christ close to home in the person of "the least of these," and Acts 1:8, where Jesus endows his followers with power to become "witnesses" in the global context.

Empowerment ethics is by no means an exclusively Christian agenda; persons of other faiths and secular humanists have also effectively concerned themselves to provide help and encouragement to those victimized by oppression and injustice. Within the African American community, however, the Christian tradition remains the premier source for moral reflection, even as it is referenced in public discourse by those outside the church. Thus the present discussion assumes that the faith affirmations and theological beliefs of the Christian tradition are a major formative source for African American life and moral reflection.

The social and ecclesial context of empowerment ethics as moral discourse is brought to the fore in this volume. African Americans in the United States can be said to be a liberated people in the sense that after five centuries of forced emigration, slavery, "Jim Crow" segregation, and discrimination in this country, at the close of the twentieth century many are experiencing increased voting rights, educational access, and economic opportunity in the wake of the civil rights movement of the 1950s and 1960s. In their contextual analyses of African American moral discourse, contemporary black liberation theologians have most often focused upon the activism of exceptional individuals during two periods of African American history: the nineteenth-century struggle against slavery (Sojourner Truth, Frederick Douglass, Harriet Tubman, Nat Turner) and the twentieth-century quest

3

for human and civil rights led by Martin Luther King, Jr., and El-Hajj Malik El-Shabazz (Malcolm X). This book envisions a somewhat broader sociohistorical perspective inclusive of the contributions of individuals and organizations who have exemplified and embodied empowerment ethics at other points in African American history. Moreover, there is a need to push the black church's historic understanding of prophetic ministry beyond the mandate articulated by liberation theologians and ethicists to respond to the plight of the poor. This is not to negate or diminish that mandate's force in any way but to underscore the church's obligation to address the ethical predicament of both rich and poor, female and male, victim and victimizer, underclass and middle class, and to challenge all to exercise their choices and dispense their resources in morally responsible ways.

Empowerment is the process by which an individual or group conveys to others the authority to act. Although empowerment finds meaningful application in politics, economics, and social relations, in this discussion it is most highly valued as a spiritual transaction that both invokes and responds to the divine presence as mediated through human interaction. To be specific, empowerment ethics means the norms, principles, and ethos ascribed to individuals and groups engaged in the task of liberating others by empowering them to act. The formulation of an ethical code for the empowered can begin with the adoption of the Golden Rule, the principle of moral reciprocity and empathy taught by Christianity and other world religions. Framed as a general guide toward empowerment for liberative praxis, the Golden Rule would be rendered something like this: as you would that others should do to you—whatever your sex, race, class, sexual preference, or however you measure your status in relation to those others—do so to them. In short, treat others as you would like to be treated if you had to trade places with them.

Seven separate approaches to empowerment are described in the chapters that follow. Each term is descriptive of a path toward empowerment that can be pursued independently of the others.

4

Alternatively, they can be understood as steps taken by an individual or group to move progressively from a state of victimization to one of moral agency within the framework of Christian faith. They reflect a chronology of collective transformation within changing contexts of victimization, beginning with the African American experience of liberation from slavery and ending with responses to the precipitous demise of the African American family and communal civility at the close of the twentieth century. While each of these seven elements will be illustrated individually with some sense of concrete historicity, they all may find simultaneous expression at those times and places where African American Christians have ventured into arenas of empowered existence. The one-word chapter headings are intended to convey the idea that these elements represent distinct windows of insight into the Christian moral sensibilities of African Americans. Together they comprise an empowerment ethics paradigm intended to foster an integrated understanding of experience, insight, and struggle, toward the end of prescribing a holistic vision of African American moral progress that is informed by past achievements, responsive to present demands, and accountable to future generations.

First is *testimony,* personal accounts of religious conversion that inspired some of the earliest autobiographical literature and other documentation of the experience of New World Africans. The conversion narratives of ex-slaves not only address the evils of oppression but also affirm the humanity of the oppressed before God.

Second, *protest* is the public outcry articulated by African American Christians on behalf of the oppressed. Based upon their discernment of the hypocrisy of the white Christian churches and society, abolitionists, civil rights activists, and intellectuals have used protest as an effective vehicle for social change.

Uplift, third, is the inwardly directed counterpart of protest, grounded in the intragroup social ethics that correspond to demands for justice pointed toward the larger society. It is the acknowledged agenda of black women's clubs and church organizations and of the Holiness churches who welcomed and embraced the poor in the cities.

Fourth is the *cooperation* that follows when individuals who have become aware of their victimized state attempt to join forces with other oppressed individuals and groups to develop strategies and goals for personal progress and community development. This has been an especially difficult imperative for African American men and women to pursue together in the churches.

Achievement refers to the fifth process, wherein efforts toward self-advancement become focused and morally meaningful for those who have affirmed their own humanity, responded critically to the evil within and without, and begun to articulate a constructive vision of their own future and what is hoped for their succeeding generations. Traditionally, education has been viewed as the key to this dimension of personal and collective empowerment. African American women have created interesting spaces for fostering church and community role models in this regard.

The term *remoralization* is introduced here to describe a sixth stage or dimension of empowerment, that is, the self-directed transformation of persons who have been demoralized by oppressive forces operating in the society and within the human psyche, toward the end of enabling them to function as socially responsible moral agents.

Ministry is the seventh and final outcome of the process. The church itself can be understood as the principal arena in which empowered individuals, families, and communities can devote their gifts and resources to serving the needs of others, consistent with the example of Jesus Christ.

The term *salvation* has been used by Christians to describe the total transformation suggested by this ethical paradigm. The strictly social understanding of sin and the entirely economic understanding of salvation characteristic of modern African American moral discourse are inadequate and misleading, especially in view of the present moral condition of African Americans, both poor and affluent. Sin is best understood as both personal and collective. In liberatory discourse the personal dimension of sin tends to collapse under the weight of the analysis of victimization, and its collective significance is reduced to an amalgam of sins of discrimination against those marginalized by their color, sex, economic status, and/or sexual preference. When salvation is equated solely with liberation, that is, with the attainment of freedom from oppression and discrimination, the moral and spiritual significance of personal formation too easily becomes obscured.

The concept of empowerment ethics addresses at least some of these problems. From the vantage point of evangelical Christianity as preached and practiced by many African Americans, salvation is an experience of individual empowerment that commences when one is challenged to embrace a higher truth and to undergo conversion. This book attempts to show how the ethical frame of reference for the spiritually empowered individual can be expanded into the interpersonal realm. There are numerous examples of empowered and empowering behaviors that promote social salvation in various ways, specifically, by protest of the conditions that caused or exacerbated the initial state of demoralization, by uplift of those who yet suffer in and from those conditions, by cooperation with others who share the same agenda for social progress, by achievement of a sense of vocation and personal fulfillment, and by ministry to the "lost" with a clear sense of one's own spiritual and social identity. "Remoralization" names the process by which persons who have been demoralized as a consequence of oppression, victimization, and self-destructive acts acquire moral agency and become positioned to make positive contributions to the moral progress of the entire community.

Empowerment ethics posits norms and principles for people in charge, people who are serious about their accountability to others in the form of justice. Dietrich Bonhoeffer, the Christian theologian who lost his life while taking a stand against Adolf

Hitler in Nazi Germany, warned against "cheap grace" in *The Cost of Discipleship*.[3] The moral predicament of some modern African American Christian intellectuals suggests a "cheap justice" of demanding repentance and restitution from the oppressing group in the name of God, without fostering a corresponding self-critique on the part of either the oppressed or those who claim to speak for them. Cheap justice is manifested in the lives of empowered individuals who verbalize prophetic claims on behalf of the oppressed, but who distance themselves physically, emotionally, and politically from the oppressed group, freely imbibing the elite privileges, status, and material benefits offered by the very same structures and networks they oppose with words. Cheap justice is a self-centered barrage of complaints giving more attention to rhetoric than to remedies, set forth by individuals whose moral and spiritual indicators have been confounded by assimilation of the same postmodern doubts and anxieties that hound the oppressor classes. Costly justice, on the other hand, is a sacrificial struggle on the part of empowered individuals who maintain creative partnerships with the oppressed and who identify unambiguously with the best interests of the oppressed group. Costly justice is grounded in the ongoing vision and work of persons whose moral outlook and spiritual principles have been forged in the communal historical experience of oppression.

In light of cheap and costly justice, the social ethics of white flight and black flight appear remarkably similar, as affluent blacks today flee the same homes, church edifices, and neighborhoods that affluent whites abandoned a generation ago, and for the same reasons—crime, substandard schools, lower property values, and so on. Then as now, there may be notable efforts on the part of white Christians to cultivate some sense of urban mission and to engage in activities to serve the needs of people in the inner cities. In view of the changing demographics of today's cities, however, few viable incentives or opportunities remain for black middle-class individuals, families, and churches who have "escaped" poor, crime-ridden neighborhoods to "give back" anything to empower those left behind. Some black urban churches are positioned to encourage ministries of liberation and empowerment designed to benefit the poor. But what is needed is the construction—or recovery, as the case may be—of a Christian ethic to guide individual Christians and churches through the task of recycling the vision of empowerment among the poor in ways that evidence both spiritual reflection and social conscience. It is hoped that this book will be a helpful resource for church and community leaders engaged in the task of bringing the Christian gospel to light in the lives of African Americans at all levels of spiritual and socioeconomic development.

Testimony

Conversion testimonies of Africans enslaved in America represent one of the earliest forms of autobiography to appear in African American literature, dating back to the second half of the eighteenth century. William L. Andrews has related this form of spiritual autobiography to the pursuit of personal freedom and spiritual empowerment:

> The black spiritual autobiographer traced his or her freedom back to the acquisition of some sort of saving knowledge and to an awakening of awareness within. The recognition of one's true identity, unfettered by either the slavery of sin or the sin of slavery, set in motion a process by which early black Christians, and later, black slaves, attained spiritual as well as secular freedom.[1]

Christian slaves who spoke with eloquence of their conversion experiences often testified also against the evil of slavery. By the antebellum period the majority of religious slaves were either Baptist or Methodist, typically having been converted at revivals, camp meetings, and other such means that flourished as conversion-oriented evangelical Protestantism swept the South. There is abundant evidence that slaves shaped their own distinctive folk religion, which combined features of evangelical Protestantism with African religious values and practices. This slave religion, often referred to as the "invisible institution," was mostly practiced in secret because the slaves' worship and prayers were focused on their desire for freedom from slavery.

One of the principal sources for the study of slave religion from the perspective of the Christian slave is the published collection of several thousand ex-slave interviews conducted during the 1930s under the sponsorship of the Federal Writers Project of the Work Projects Administration.[2] Some of these oral histories were collected a decade earlier through the special research projects of black institutions of higher learning, such as Fisk University and Hampton Institute. From these invaluable sources it is possible to gain insight into the spiritual empowerment and social ethics of the slaves. Much of the available testimony documents how religious experience fueled the slaves' moral outrage in response to slavery.

[handwritten margin note: First-hand accounts]

Ethics and Eschatology in Slave Christianity

The slaves adopted a variety of ethical styles in relation to the problem of slavery.[3] If a distinctive element is present in their collective ethical reflections, it would be their almost unanimous refusal to defend slavery on the ground of Christian ethics. In a sense, every conversion experience is a highly individualized phenomenon; however, the social ethical orientation of the slaves toward freedom derives directly from the fact that slavery was an experience of shared suffering. For the ex-slave, conversion is what happened to "me," while slavery is what happened to "us." The empowerment to moral agency brought about by the conversion experience was felt in both the personal and social aspects of slave existence.

In the Bible, conversion means turning away from sin and wrongfulness and turning toward God and righteousness. The conversion experience typically includes both passive and active elements—a passive acceptance of sanctification and an active response to the commission to serve and evangelize others. The ambiguous relationship between the passive and active components of conversion replicates itself in the ethical dilemma the convert faces in seeking to live righteously in an evil world: Should the convert play a role of passive acceptance or active response when confronted by unrighteous structures, forces, and persons? What should one do in situations where the passive stance implies waiting for God to act, while the active posture assumes that God awaits human action? In particular, the dilemma of the convert who is a slave is a question of how to confront the evil of slavery—by enduring bondage patiently until God brings into reality a new age of freedom, or by taking the initiative to escape or overthrow the oppressive system?

In their clandestine prayer meetings, held late at night in the slave quarters and hush harbors, the slaves participated in the transforming power of the age for which they hoped by petitioning God for deliverance from bondage. They believed that the same God who transformed the sinful status of their souls in the conversion experience would transform the sinful structures of the society. The God who had freed their souls from sin could certainly free their bodies from slavery. In the meantime, and perhaps in a manner more in keeping with the ethical traditions of biblical people than modern Christians can fully appreciate, the slave church embodied what ethicist Tom Ogletree has identified as the fundamental dialectic of eschatological existence: "on the one hand, accommodating oneself to the setting of one's calling; on the other hand, acting congruently with the promise of Christian freedom."[4] One post-emancipation interpretation of the eschatological significance of the experience of slavery conveys a firm conviction that the hope, patience, and endurance of the slave community were finally vindicated:

> I 'members 'bout the days of slavery and I don't 'lieve they ever gwine have slaves no more on this earth. I think Gawd done took

Religious Experience plus primary source for ethics, not scripture. Are legally enforced illiteracy.

Testimony

that burden offen his black chillun and I'm aiming to praise him for it to his face in the days of Glory what ain't so far off.[5]

The religion of the Christian slaves is striking in its adaptation of biblical ethics and eschatology, drawing its authority directly from religious experience and only derivatively from knowledge of biblical texts. Legally enforced illiteracy prevented the masses of slaves from gaining individual access to the teachings and traditions of the Bible, but the conversion experience inscribed its essential message in their enraptured hearts. Otherwise, the slaves might have believed the misconstrued gospel of submission their masters preached, had preached to them, or forced them to preach to each other. But not even the most obsequious of slaves seemed to acquiesce in the notion that God willed their bondage and subservience to whites. Instead, the slaves embraced the dynamic gospel of freedom that was preached, taught, and practiced in the quarters. There were Christians within the slave community who struggled with the same dilemma faced by generations of biblical peoples before them, weighing their own powerlessness over against the superior force of a destructive and alienating social order in an effort to determine whether it is better to wait or to act, to pray or to fight. There were Christian slaves who waited and prayed, and others who resisted and fought; all claimed to be moved by religious convictions in choosing which course to pursue.

Situation Ethics: Stealing and Lying

The oral histories of the former slaves illumine the impact of racial considerations on the social ethics of these Christians in chains. In particular, their response to the brutal immorality and hypocritical behavior of whites became a dominant factor in the process of moral reasoning with regard to behaviors such as stealing and lying, and shaped their understanding of the larger questions concerning the morality of religion and the justice of God.

Stealing is one of the morally questionable behaviors most

13

frequently mentioned in the ex-slave materials. Slaves confessed to stealing chickens, eggs, hogs, and other foodstuffs from their own and neighboring plantations, often with the explanation that they were forced to steal in order to have enough to eat. In his autobiography *Up from Slavery*, Booker T. Washington shares a childhood remembrance from slavery when his mother awakened him and his siblings in the middle of the night to eat a chicken that she had secured from some unknown source:

> Some people may call this theft. If such a thing were to happen now, I should condemn it as theft myself. But taking place at the time it did, and for the reason that it did, no one could ever make me believe that my mother was guilty of thieving. She was simply a victim of the system of slavery.[6]

Ex-slave informants were very forthright in asserting several justifications for theft. Foremost is the claim that stealing was a necessary response under conditions of malnourishment: "How could they help but steal, when they didn't have nothin'? You didn't eat if you didn't steal."[7] Another ex-slave provides a carefully reasoned explanation for this behavior in view of the gross inequities of the slave system:

> I did not regard it as stealing then, I do not regard it as such now. I hold that a slave has a moral right to eat and drink and wear all that he needs, and that it would be a sin on his part to suffer and starve in a country where there is plenty to eat and wear within his reach. I consider that I had a just right to what I took, because it was the labor of my hands.[8]

The situation ethics set forth by some of these informants tended to justify the theft of material necessities on the grounds that they had been victimized by a much worse crime, namely, the theft of human persons: "Dey allus tell us it am wrong to lie and steal, but why did de white folks steal my mammy and her mammy? Dat de sinfulles' stealin' dey is."[9] One ex-slave recalls exposing the hypocrisy and immoral example of whites in this regard in a confrontation with his master: "I told my master one day—said I, 'You white folks set the bad example of stealing—you stole us from Africa, and not content with that, if any get free here, you stole them afterward, and so we are made slaves.'"[10] Ironically, the slaves were made both victims and unwitting collaborators in the white slaveholders' crimes of theft: "It wuz funny, de white folks would whip de niggers for stealin', but if dey saw a hog in de woods, dey would make de niggers catch de hog and kill him and hide him under dey bushes."[11]

An alternative ethic arose also with respect to lying. In his comprehensive study of slave religion, Albert J. Raboteau notes that "lying and deceit, normally considered moral vices, were virtues to slaves in their dealings with whites."[12] This radical reversal in moral reasoning was fueled by the basic conviction that the only morally appropriate response to the deception and depravity of slaveholders was to make every effort not to fulfill the ultimate objective of their efforts, that is, to produce hard-working, honest, and submissive slaves. Moreover, it was important to discern and implement a different moral code in relation to whites based upon their negative moral status in the eyes of the slaves. William Wells Brown once stated that the slaves on his plantation "were always glad to shirk labor and thought that to deceive whites was a religious duty."[13]

The ethics of stealing from thieves and deceiving the deceivers was empowering for these slaves insofar as they contextualized their thought and behavior with respect to a religious duty to undermine an unjust social order. In fact, the slaves' moral sense led them to define wrong in terms of white moral norms, where white attitudes and conduct were lifted up as counterexamples of what was acceptable in the slave community: "a slave that will steal from a slave is called *mean as master*. This is the lowest comparison slaves know how to use: 'just as mean as white folks.'"[14] The slaves did not tolerate stealing and lying among themselves, because such behavior would constitute an imitation of white immorality to the detriment of black solidarity and well-being. It is clearly evident that the slaves fashioned a moral double standard with one set of norms applied to their own group and another to their interaction with whites. This double standard can be viewed as two aspects of a single moral code derived from a combination of social, religious, and racial considerations. The rule of mutual solidarity in the slave community and the notion of the right of slaves to the products of their own work both exemplify a situational empowerment ethics. The moral code of the slaves was partly sanctioned by the everyday social experience of the community, and in part by the Christian religion and the communal ethos rooted in their African past.[15] To be sure, some slaves adhered to the Christian morality that precluded all stealing, lying, and sabotage, which may have worked for the benefit of the slaveholder. But at the same time these intragroup prohibitions also worked for the good of the slave community by preventing internal conflict. It is important to observe that in general the slaves exhibited a profound respect for the principles of justice, and in most cases took care not to "turn the tables" against their oppressors by returning evil for evil. Paul Escott has concluded from his analysis of the ex-slave interviews that the slave community was governed by an ethic of justice, as opposed to the master's system of right and wrong:

> This ethic permitted "theft" but imposed its own constraints. The former slaves believed it was right to take what was theirs; they plainly did not feel that it was right to turn the tables and inflict great harm on the master, thus causing injustice to flow in the opposite direction.[16]

This ethic of justice exemplifies the extent to which a Christian community can be empowered in its responses to adverse social conditions without assimilating the moral perverseness of the oppressors, thereby affirming an ancient biblical admonition, "Do not envy the violent man, and do not choose any of his ways; for the perverse are an abomination to the Lord, but the upright are in his confidence" (Prov. 3:31-32).

White Christian Hypocrisy

In their religious testimony the slaves frequently condemn the hypocrisy of white religion. Just as the slaves shaped their moral code regarding theft and lying in response to the negative examples set by whites, so also did they define their own religion as the antithesis of the religion of the slaveholder. Escott finds the former slaves' open scorn for white religion to be one of the most consistent and vehement themes in the narratives.[17] In the judgment of some, the idea of a good Christian slaveholder was a moral impossibility:

> Some folks say slaveholders may be good Christians, but I can't and won't believe it, nor do I think that a slaveholder can get to heaven. He may possibly get there, I don't know; but though I wish to get there myself, I don't want to have anything more to do with slaveholders either here or in heaven.[18]

The slaves were especially critical of white preachers, many of whom were hired by plantation owners to preach a religion that sanctioned slavery. The Southern white evangelical defense of slavery on biblical grounds was widely regarded as a joke, and caused some to reject the religious authority of the Bible. With or without scriptural verification, the "theology of slavery" was an untenable concept in the moral perspective of those who suffered under its allegedly divine curse. The slaves saw no truth in the sermons of whites, and resented the fact that white preachers were primarily concerned with admonishing them to be good slaves: "You ought to heared that preachin'. Obey your massa and missy, but nary a word 'bout having a soul to save."[19] The slaves knew better than to take seriously the white preachers who sought to use religion and biblical hermeneutics to justify and support the institution of slavery. No elaborate polemics or carefully constructed moral arguments were required to convince the slaves that there was a fundamental discrepancy between their social status as slaves and the will of God for human life and destiny.

One fugitive slave attested to the slaves' basic ability to discern that slavery itself was morally wrong, despite the claims of white preachers and theologians: "I have heard poor ignorant slaves, that did not know A from B, say that they did not believe the Lord ever intended they should be slaves, and that they did not see how it should be so."[20] There were times, ironically enough, when the slaves were able to hear their own slaveholders make deathbed confessions of the sin of slaveholding and ask their forgiveness for injustices done to them. The narratives make mention of the slaves' conviction that slaveholders, particularly the "mean" ones, were destined to be eternally punished in hell for the crimes done against blacks. The fact that the narratives do not convey the notion of an all-white hell or an all-black heaven indicates that the slaves discerned, eschatologically speaking, that God was not a respecter of persons in doling out eternal punishments and rewards.

Theodicy

Regarding the question of theodicy, most moral statements made in the narratives about the evil of slavery are closely connected with a belief in a just God. Their ethic of justice rested squarely on the theological presupposition that God would act to free the slaves based on the precedent set in the Scriptures when God freed Israel from bondage in Egypt. Moreover, this ethic was also closely connected with the slaves' affirmation of their own God-given humanity. Their anthropology contradicted the theology of slavery and the perverted social order that sought to secure their status as property and not as fully human persons. Indeed, the anthropological assumptions, theological questions, and moral affirmations of the slaves were deeply rooted in their contextual approaches to biblical interpretation: "We poor creatures have need to believe in God, for if God Almighty will not be good to us some day, why were we born? When I heard of his delivering his people from bondage I know it means the poor African."[21]

This testimony claims the past history of God's goodness and omnipotence for the Africans in exile in America. In this view, divine intervention on behalf of the slave is a necessary justification of the existence of the slave and of God.

There is evidence that some slaves rejected the notion of God altogether on the logic that if God existed "he wouldn't let white folks do as they have done for so many years."[22] Notwithstanding the success or failure of the theodicy argument, the slaves' discernment of the fundamental discrepancy between their own views of humanity and the dehumanizing effects of slavery served as their primary frame of ethical reference. A social ethic based on a distinctive religious ethic provided the criteria against which a broad range of moral judgments were made to establish ground rules for both intragroup relations and dealings with whites. The fundamental truth affirmed in slave testimony was that God created them to be free and responsible moral agents in a just society; the primary lie they negated was the slaveholding principle that one person could possess and control another as personal property. Their religious ethics served the purposes of a just God who mandated the implementation of justice. They regarded the entire experience of slavery as a temporary moral aberration that would soon be corrected by divine and human action within the social order, guided by religious and social ethics.

Emancipation

Eventually, of course, all the slaves were indeed emancipated, irrespective of whether they had accommodated themselves to bondage or had struggled to set themselves free. Emancipation was celebrated as a time for giving thanks to God for bringing the long-sought day of deliverance to fulfillment. But what did emancipation mean to the Christian ex-slaves? Did it bring an end to their protracted struggle against evil in the society? Did emancipation occasion liberation and empowerment, or did it inspire further means of oppression and victimization?

Excerpts from the interviews of four ex-slave women who commented on the subject of freedom demonstrate how the ex-slaves' sense of empowerment changed in concert with the times and circumstances in the aftermath of slavery. The first informant, Miss Catherine of Nashville, Tennessee, describes the meaning of freedom expressed in the religious testimony of the slaves prior to emancipation: "Well, they'd say the Lord showed 'em where they was free and they got up and told us about it; tell anybody, and everybody; that's the way anybody'll do when yo' soul done been set free, ain't it?"[23] For the slave Christians, the meaning of freedom was enmeshed in the tension between the "already" and the "not yet"—already revealed in the soul but not yet experienced in the flesh. Nevertheless, it is evident that the irrepressible testimonies of those whom the Lord set free proved to be a real source of encouragement for the congregations of slaves who had prayed secretly for liberation from bondage, understood as the physical and social counterpart of the spiritual freedom they openly confessed and claimed for their souls. What is especially empowering about this assertion that "the Lord showed 'em where they was free and they got up and told us about it" is the realization that the content of these testimonies was derived from spiritual ways of knowing, a revealed knowledge declared with prophetic boldness.

A second informant, Mary Ellen Johnson of Dallas, Texas, recalls her conflicting thoughts and feelings as a child seeking understanding of the meaning of emancipation:

> They tell me that the war is over and that I am going to be raised free and that I don't b'long to nobuddy but God and my mammy and pappy. After that they used to tell me all the time that I am free but it don't make me see or feel nothing 'cause I ain't never know I ain't free. But they say, Remember you is free.[24]

Once emancipation came, it was necessary for the newly freed slaves to teach and remind each other of the meaning of freedom, as revealed in Johnson's poignant childhood memories of her own orientation to freedom. Obviously, her parents intended to instill within her an appreciation for freedom, even if the full impact of this changed status was difficult for her to comprehend. Significantly, she was told she was no longer the property of any slaveholder, but "belonged" only to God and her parents. This new understanding and experience of belonging bears the marks of the social and religious ethics of the African American Christian community of slaves.

A third informant, Virginia Harris of Coahoma County, Mississippi, speaks of some of the shortcomings, limitations, and benefits of freedom:

> Me and my husband farmed all our married life. We was told we was to get forty acres and a mule. Nobody ain't got nothing, as I seed, 'cept freedom to come and go when you please. Compelled to be better off that way. When you is in bondage, you ain't got no more chance than a bull frog.[25]

Obviously, the ebullience of the emancipation experience was tempered by the ex-slaves' realization that they would not be given the promised acreage and draft animals to enable them to earn a living for themselves. Still, freedom was better than bondage in that it provided more life chances. The freed slaves soon came to understand two dimensions of freedom—release from old securities and dependencies on the one hand, and taking on new risks and responsibilities on the other.

A fourth informant, Mrs. Hannah Davidson of Toledo, Ohio, discusses freedom and forgiveness of the wrongs done to her while a slave in light of her understanding of the teachings of Christ:

> I never got a penny. My master kept me and my sister Mary twenty-two long years after we were supposed to be free. Work, work, work. I don't think my sister and I ever went to bed before twelve o'clock at night. . . .
> Well, slavery's over and I think that's a grand thing. A white lady recently asked me, "Don't you think you were better off under the

white people?" I said, "What you talkin' about? The birds of the air have their freedom." I don't know why she should ask me that anyway.

I belong to the Third Baptist Church. I think all people should be religious. Christ was a missionary. He went about doing good to people. You should be clean, honest, and do everything good for people. I first turn the searchlight on myself. To be a true Christian, you must do as Christ said: "Love one another." You know, that's why I said I didn't want to tell about my life and the terrible things that I and my sister Mary suffered. I want to forgive those people. Some people tell me those people are in hell now. But I don't think that. I believe we should all do good to everybody.[26]

Countless slaves, like Hannah Davidson, were continually deceived and deprived of their right to freedom and wages long after slavery ended. For some of the ex-slaves who were Christians, however, the meaning of freedom included release from psychological and spiritual bondage to bitter memories. In an effort to hold herself accountable to her own view of a true Christian as a follower of Christ's commandment to "love one another," Davidson feels compelled to forget her suffering and forgive her oppressors, even to the point of refusing to let her own testimony of abuse and deception serve as grounds for consigning them to hell. True freedom, like true forgiveness, rests upon the confidence that whatever is loosed on earth is loosed also in heaven.

Freedom thus bore a plethora of meanings in the thought and experience of African Americans as they made their transition out of bondage. Emancipation did not bring an end to the black Christians' struggle against evil in the society, but rather introduced new dimensions and challenges to that struggle. Ironically, it takes the testimony of the ex-slave to illustrate fully the meaning of the gospel of freedom in its most dramatic proportions. The collective experience of the ex-slaves recalls an ancient religious metaphor described by historian David Brion Davis in *Slavery and Human Progress:*

To become a "slave" to Yahweh or Christ was not simply to imitate the humility and subservience of a bondsman. It was also to acknowledge the transference of primal loyalties and obligations to a new and awesome power, in the hope of gaining a new and transcendent freedom.[27]

Religion and Morality in the Aftermath of Slavery

The post-emancipation religion of the African American Christians underwent changes in concert with the ex-slaves' changing understanding of the meaning of freedom and empowerment. Many of those who shared their oral histories in the 1920s and 1930s testified to the demise of the religion of the slave quarters, and at the same time lamented the shallow spirituality and moral laxity of what was then the current generation of African American Christians. In general, the ex-slaves relate the peculiar character of the "old-time religion" to the suffering and ignorance they endured as slaves. Before emancipation, slaves were more willing to shout and to make sincere professions of religion. By contrast, contemporary black Christians were thought to be more enlightened and sophisticated, but less fervent in belief.

Shouting, or ecstatic religious dance, was viewed as a sign of grace in slave religion, but was apparently rejected and ridiculed by a more sophisticated generation of young Christians:

> I still shouts at meetings. I don't have nothing to do with it. It hits me jest like a streak of lightning and there ain't no holding it. I goes now to the camp meetings close to Karnack [Texas] and trys to behave, but when I gets in the Spirit, jest can't hold that shouting back. The young fo'ks make fun of me, but I don't mind. Style is crowded all the grace out of religion today.[28]

Thus, attention to style "has crowded all the grace out of religion." Evidently style was not a concern in the old-time religion, and grace was received with a joyous sense of abandon. A second informant observed that the content of religion may have remained the same, but a measure of moral integrity has definitely been lost:

> In them days the people professed religion just like they do now, but they was more ignorant, and yet I sometimes think they was more honest and sincere than they are now.[29]

A third statement suggests that there is a negative correlation between education and belief, a situation exacerbated by evidence that the younger blacks are misusing their increased access to education and knowledge:

> The young Negroes don't believe things we believe forty and fifty years ago. When I was a boy I got religion, and really got converted. "Sociality" is taking the world today. Course we got more education 'mong the Negroes now than when I was a boy, but I don't think they is using it right, or there wouldn't be so many in the penitentiary. I think the young race of Negroes is in a bad fix if they ain't some change.[30]

In other words, the meaning of religion is lost when worshipers concentrate on "sociality," that is, trivial social matters, and neglect the weightier matters of faith and life.

Thus the transition from the old to the new styles of religious expression is tied to a decline in morality. The so-called invisible institution had maintained its social ethical focus on the need for deliverance from suffering and ignorance; both the ecstasy and the prayers of slaves at worship reflected an utter reliance upon God's ability to transform human hearts and social conditions. But after emancipation, the social ethical focus became somewhat blurred, and African American Christianity began to take on some of the socially irresponsible characteristics of its white evangelical counterpart. Throughout the slaveholding era, white Christians had crafted biblical and theological justifications for slavery. Once slavery had ended, the theology, social ethics, and biblical hermeneutics of white Christians who supported the continued subjugation and oppression of blacks became increas-

ingly devoid of social content, mainly because their racist practices were morally and biblically indefensible. Henceforth, the social ethical witness of the black and white churches would wax
and wane under conditions of strict racial segregation throughout the twentieth century.

The religious testimony of the former slaves should be read as
a graphic illustration of the most critical hermeneutical challenge
facing Bible-believing Christians, namely, the struggle to be faithful to God's call to freedom and justice in the midst of a society
that offers attractive compromises with the evils of oppression.
There were Christian slaves, not only in the big houses but also
in the fields, who found a strange level of comfort and security in
their chains. There were those who humbly submitted to the social security of white patronage and etiquette in the Jim Crow
South. But these African American Christians found themselves
in the same moral position as the oppressed people that Moses,
the Hebrew prophets, Jesus, and Paul taught and led and rebuked
in biblical times. In the Bible, the key to the liberation and empowerment of the people was their willingness to become converted and to accept the divine commission to call others to par-
ticipate in the new age of God's reign and restoration. For many
slaves whose testimonies of conversion to Christianity affirmed
their humanity before God and the worshiping community, spiritual empowerment occasioned also prayerful participation in the
pursuit of freedom and justice.

Protest

A long-standing tradition of African American Christians is protest of slavery and other forms of racial oppression. Some of these critiques have focused attention on "external" factors such as slavery, racially motivated violence, and discrimination in education and employment, in an effort to account for the problems and lack of progress of African Americans. Others have examined these same problems and lack of progress by pointing to "internal" factors such as ignorance, racial disunity, and failure to pursue existing educational and employment opportunities. In general, advocates of the external critique have been labeled "liberals," and advocates of the internal critique have been called "conservatives." Both the liberal and conservative critics hold that freedom is the key to the progress or well-being of African Americans. In an interesting reversal of what normally distinguishes liberal from conservative in mainstream American social and political thought, the African American liberals tend to emphasize freedom in its negative sense, that is, freedom *from* interference or coercion, while the conservatives emphasize freedom in its positive sense, that is, freedom *to* be or to do what one chooses.

The legacy of liberal protest, with its emphasis upon freedom *from,* is identified with the push for civil rights, and the conservative critique, with its emphasis upon freedom *to,* is identified with civil responsibility. Any ethical evaluation of the African American situation in American life should incorporate both dimensions of the problems and progress of blacks, that is, the pursuit of civil rights and the exercise of civil responsibility. If rights are understood as that which is due to anyone by law, tradition, or nature, and responsibility is personal accountability or ability to act without guidance or superior authority, then the moral feasibility of asserting rights without assuming responsibility, or, conversely, of appropriating responsibility in the absence of rights, is readily brought into question. Moreover, at issue is the debate over whether the same or a separate standard of morality is applicable to whites and blacks with respect to the normative influences that determine behavior, such as values, social norms, and personal attitudes. The most helpful ethical critiques seem to be those that assume a single standard of social ethics for all races and groups, or that at least apply the same moral norms and judgments to one's own race or group as to others.

Two of the most important protest documents of the antebellum period were produced by free black Christian abolitionists living in the North: David Walker's *Appeal to the Coloured Citizens of the World,* originally published in 1829, and Maria Steward's "Religion and the Pure Principles of Morality," dated 1831.[1] Both statements situate their complaint against America in the context of Christian ethics. Moreover, they each address the external and internal aspects of the African American moral predicament, that is, naming the sins of whites and blacks according to a single standard of biblical morality. Three major questions will guide evaluation of these protest documents: (1) What is the author's self-identified role in relation to the black community? (2) what is the author's vision of black moral progress? and (3) what solutions are proposed to achieve this progress? In addition, attention will be given to assumptions concerning the concepts of freedom, rights, and responsibility, and the question of who sets the standards for black and white behavior. An assessment will be made of the implications of these nineteenth-century protest speeches for the ongoing articulation of empowerment ethics and theological social criticism in view of the oppressive conditions imposed upon African Americans from this nation's inception.

David Walker's *Appeal*

David Walker's *Appeal* is addressed to the "coloured citizens of the world." He believed he was sent by God upon a divine mission of advocacy for the masses of slaves and free blacks. Walker was born in 1785 in North Carolina to a free mother and a slave father. Having inherited the free status of his mother, he acquired a good education and traveled extensively along the Eastern seaboard. Eventually he established himself as a used-clothing dealer in Boston, Massachusetts, where he was actively involved in the abolitionist movement as a lecturer, writer, and agent for an abolitionist newspaper. Walker was found dead in the doorway of his Boston shop in June 1830, a few days after publishing the *Appeal* in its third edition. The exact cause of his death was never determined; however, it is generally believed that he was murdered.[2]

In Walker's view, the key problem of blacks in antebellum America was slavery and the racist ideology of black inferiority that undergirded it. He explores several dimensions of the problem, including widespread ignorance and poor employment opportunities resulting from systematic efforts on the part of whites to withhold education and economic advancement from blacks, the failure of blacks to resist being held as slaves, and the hypocrisy of white Christians who supported and participated in the abuse and degradation of blacks. The critique is both external and internal in scope; moral responsibility for the condition of blacks in America is actually attributed to slave and slaveholder alike. Walker condemns slaveholders for failing to respect the human rights and dignity of the slave, and at the same time he condemns slaves for failing to employ whatever means would be necessary to secure their own human rights and dignity.

Walker's vision of black progress is a messianic vision of a "united and happy America" where there is reconciliation between the races and a relationship of mutual respect. His prescription for black progress calls for action on the part of whites to bring slavery and oppression to an end:

> Throw away your fears and prejudices then, and enlighten us and treat us like men, and we will like you more than we do now hate you, and tell us now no more about colonization, for America is as much our country as it is yours.—Treat us like men, and there is no danger but that we will all live in peace and happiness together.[3]

Walker's prescription for black progress also calls for action on the part of blacks to unite in order to emancipate themselves from oppression:

> I advance it therefore to you, not as a *problematical,* but as an unshaken and forever immovable *fact,* that your full glory and happiness, as well as all other coloured people under heaven, shall never be fully consummated, but with the *entire emancipation of your enslaved brethren all over the world.* You may therefore, go to work and do what you can to rescue, or join in with tyrants to oppress them and yourselves, until the Lord shall come upon you all like a thief in the night. . . . Remember, to let the aim of your labours among your brethren, and particularly the youths, be the dissemination of education and religion.[4]

The effort to emancipate and educate the slaves, then, is the work of God, who will bring not only glory to the oppressed but also judgment to their oppressors.

Walker's self-help ethic applies a single standard for behavior and social responsibility to both blacks and whites. It is informed by three biblical texts: (1) the declaration that God has no respect of persons (Acts 10:34-36), (2) the Golden Rule (Matt. 7:12), and (3) the Great Commission (Matt. 28:18-20). In the first instance, God's attributes of impartiality and justice lead to the conclusion that God is intolerant of prejudice and injustice, and is supportive of human efforts to eradicate these social evils. Second, he claims that the Golden Rule, "as you would that others do to you, so do to them," is violated by every slaveholder who mistreats others by holding them in bondage. Walker develops an interesting application of the Golden Rule to the situation of the slave, however, seeing it as obligating them to protect and defend themselves from mistreatment. His rendering of the Golden Rule for slaves would read something like this: "Don't take the abuse from others that you would not expect them to take from you." Third, the Great Commission bears the commandment to "teach all nations," based upon the assumption that all human groups are equal with regard to spiritual needs and potential. Walker seems to understand his own cause as a faithful discharge of the Great Commission, and he commends it to others as a moral imperative to emancipate, educate, and evangelize the oppressed.

Walker views freedom as a natural right, and claims that it is the responsibility of the individual to secure this freedom. In his discussion of freedom, rights, and responsibilities, he cites the Declaration of Independence as an authoritative source:

> See your declaration, Americans!! Do you understand your own language? Hear your language, proclaimed to the world, July 4, 1776—"We hold these truths to be self evident—that ALL MEN ARE CREATED EQUAL! that *they are endowed by their Creator with certain unalienable rights: that among these are life, liberty and the pursuit of happiness!!* Compare your own language above, extracted from your Declaration of Independence, with your own cruelties and murders inflicted by your cruel and unmerciful fathers and yourselves on our fathers and on us—men who have never given your fathers or you the least provocation!!!!![5]

Walker argues his appeal to natural rights based upon the logic of natural law discourse. He assumes a single ethical standard of behavior and social responsibility for both blacks and whites, but he directs much of his moral discourse specifically toward men. His use of exclusive male language seems intended to underscore the assumption that since white men have taken the lead in perpetrating atrocities against black men, black men will seek justice by violent means, acting on behalf of themselves and their women and children.

Maria Steward: Spirituality and Self-Help

Maria W. Steward (also Stewart) was born Maria Miller in Hartford, Connecticut in 1803. She was orphaned at the age of five, and was bound out to a clergyman's family. She was deprived of educational opportunity while serving this family, so at age 15 she left them to pursue her own education in Sabbath schools. In 1826 she married James W. Steward, who left her a widow in 1829. Having been cheated out of her husband's inheritance by unscrupulous lawyers, she began to earn a living by writing and public speaking. It is evident from her writings and speeches that she greatly admired fellow Bostonian David Walker. Steward is generally acknowledged as the first American-born woman of any race to speak in public, yet she left Boston in 1833 in response to censuring accusations and criticisms heaped upon her by other blacks. She traveled to New York, then to Baltimore, and finally to Washington, D. C. In 1871 she bought a building in Washington for $200 and opened a Sabbath school for seventy-five children, enlisting the help of volunteers from Howard University, where she was also employed as a matron at Freedman's Hospital. She died eight years later in 1879.[6]

Steward addresses the problems of blacks in antebellum America in an essay entitled "Religion and the Pure Principles of Morality, the Sure Foundation on Which We Must Build," published in Boston in 1831. In this essay she attributes the suffering of Africans in America to the prevalence of sin, which is primarily manifested among them in the form of ignorance and powerlessness:

Righteousness exalteth a nation, but sin is a reproach to any people. Why is it, my friends, that our minds have been blinded by ignorance, to the present moment? 'Tis on account of sin. Why is it that our church is involved in so much difficulty? 'Tis on account of sin. Why is it that God has cut down, upon our right hand and upon our left, the most learned and intelligent of our men? O, shall I say, it is on account of sin! Why is it that thick darkness is mantled upon every brow, and we, as it were, look sadly upon one another? It is on account of sin.[7]

Slavery, murder and the sexual subjugation of black women are specifically identified as sins of white America:

Oh, America, America, foul and indelible is thy stain! Dark and dismal is the cloud that hangs over thee, for thy cruel wrongs and injuries to the fallen sons of Africa. The blood of her murdered ones cries to heaven for vengeance against thee. Thou art almost become drunken with the blood of her slain; thou hast enriched thyself through her toils and labours; and now thou refuseth to make even a small return. And thou hast caused the daughters of Africa to commit whoredoms and fornications; but upon thee be their curse.[8]

She extends the scope of her protest to the global sphere, with the complaint that the United States has refused diplomatic acknowledgment of Haiti, which, at the time, was the only independent black nation in the Western Hemisphere. Using the African nomenclature to signify the African identity of the oppressed masses of black slaves in the United States, she prayerfully invokes the wrath of God against America with reference to the ten plagues of Egypt:

You may kill, tyrannize, and oppress as much as you choose, until our cry shall come up before the throne of God; for I am firmly persuaded, that he will not suffer you to quell the proud, fearless and undaunted spirits of the Africans forever; for in his own time, he is able to plead our cause against you, and to pour out upon you the ten plagues of Egypt.[9]

American Civil War

Steward devotes a great deal more attention to internal prescriptions for black progress than to analysis of black problems when addressing herself directly to blacks. Like Walker, she presents a self-help ethic that emphasizes black unity, but her distinctive application of this ethic is in terms of the roles of women in three key institutions within the black community—families, schools, and businesses. Steward ascribes to mothers primary responsibility for the moral development of children, charging them to "create in the minds of your little girls and boys a thirst for knowledge, the love of virtue, the abhorrence of vice, and the cultivation of a pure heart."[10] She proposes that women unite outside the home to establish schools and businesses:

> Let every female heart become united, and let us raise a fund ourselves; and at the end of one year and a half, we might be able to lay the corner-stone for the building of a high school, that the higher branches of knowledge might be enjoyed by us, and God would raise us up, and enough to aid us in our laudable designs. . . .
>
> How long shall the fair daughters of Africa be compelled to bury their mind and talents beneath a load of iron pots and kettles? Until union, knowledge and love begin to flow amongst us. . . . Do you ask, What can we do? Unite, and build a store of your own, if you cannot procure a license. Fill one side with dry goods, and the other with groceries. Do you ask, where is the money? We have spent more than enough for nonsense, to do what building we should want.[11] — *Archbishop Vista Onyibu*

Steward's vision of black progress rests upon the notion that blacks possess the same "independent spirit" as their white oppressors, but without the same inclination to violence. Unlike Walker, she rejects violence as a morally valid response to oppression: "Far be it from me to recommend to you either to kill, burn or destroy. But I would strongly recommend to you to improve your talents: let not one be buried in the earth."[12] Her advice to blacks to pursue a self-help ethic in partial imitation of their American oppressors suggests that she envisions a single standard of behavior and social responsibility for both groups. While Steward affirms that vengeance belongs exclusively to God, at the same time she encourages blacks to claim their rights in America and to demonstrate their intellect and independence to the world. She believes that by supplementing their prayers for deliverance with perseverance in knowledge, self-improvement, and virtue, blacks will ultimately merit God's deliverance from oppression: "Let nothing be lacking on your part; and, in God's own time, and his time is certainly the best, he will surely deliver you with a mighty hand and with an outstretched arm."[13] In contrast to Walker's challenge to black men to defend themselves and their families by use of violence, she fails to delineate what direct role blacks will play in the administration of justice, aside from prayer and self-improvement.

Protest and Debate:
Black Christian Intellectuals
in the Twentieth Century

Easily the dominant voice of black Christian protest in the twentieth century is Martin Luther King, Jr. His sermons and speeches advocating for civil rights have been seared upon the American public conscience, and his mass movement for social change produced an unprecedented impact upon the laws and practices in the United States having a direct bearing upon the freedom and economic empowerment of the African American people. King's writings, especially "Letter from Birmingham Jail," *Stride Toward Freedom,* and *Where Do We Go From Here,* have attained classic status in the field of Christian social ethics. Moreover, the preoccupation of contemporary African American male ethicists and theologians with the study and analysis of King's nonviolent social ethics has resulted in the production of articles and monographs that are widely read and often cited in academic circles.[14]

Based upon the assumption of general familiarity with the basic tenets and implications of King's protest writings, then, it would seem appropriate to divert attention to two divergent intellectual responses to the tradition of black protest in the post-King era as set forth by Glenn C. Loury and Cornel West.

Glenn C. Loury, who has taught political economics at Harvard and Boston University, is one of the foremost representatives of black conservative thought in the twentieth century. He identifies poverty and dependency as the key problems facing African Americans today and has been extremely critical of the protest orientation of the modern civil rights "establishment." Instead of analyzing black problems in terms of external and internal factors, Loury collapses his social critique into a list of major impediments to the achievement of black self-sufficiency, including: elected officials at state and local levels who promote "Great Society" schemes in an era of huge deficits; radical feminists, gay rights activists, environmentalists, and left-wing apologists who use public protest on behalf of the poor as a platform for their own interests; the failure of blacks to monitor the performance of black elected officials; and the development of misdirected and misinformed social policies based upon the miscalculation of black capabilities. In 1986 he published "A Prescription for Black Progress" in *The Christian Century*, which advocates a self-help approach to social and economic development:

> The great challenge facing black America today is the task of taking control of its own future by exerting the necessary leadership, making the required sacrifices, and building the needed institutions so that black social and economic development becomes a reality. No matter how windy the debate becomes among white liberals and conservatives as to what should be done, meeting this self-creating challenge ultimately depends on black action.[15]

This self-help approach has one critical component, namely, the belief that middle-class blacks are responsible to serve as advocates for poor blacks by providing means for the poor to help themselves develop to their full potential. Loury insists that poor black people have the ability to make fundamental improvements in their lives, given the opportunity. In his view, poverty is more an outcome than a cause of the kind of social behavior that produces high rates of male unemployment and incarceration, unwed pregnancy, especially among teenagers, and family instability in the nation's inner cities. Loury accuses the black middle class and its civil rights leadership of giving too much attention to the struggle against the "enemy without," while the "enemy within" goes unchecked. In other words, blacks have erred by failing to address internally the moral shortcomings of the black community with the same degree of candor and energy with which they have addressed the external critique of racism and discrimination in the society at large.

Loury's vision of black success is the eradication of black poverty in a context of pride, self-respect, and respect of others. The means he proposes to achieve this success encompasses both economics and ethics. His economic proposals are in accord with the 1980s Bush-Reagan economic agenda, for instance, urban enterprise zones, a sub-minimum wage for black youths, and tenant ownership of public housing. His ethical proposals call for the development of moral leadership within the black community. He would enlist middle-class blacks to foster hope and self-confidence in the lower classes of blacks, mainly by demonstrating that black survival requires the recognition and exploitation of economic opportunity. According to Loury, black intellectuals and political leaders should teach their people to internalize responsibility, rather than to externalize it by means of traditional civil rights protests.

With respect to freedom, rights, and responsibility, Loury believes that the legal struggle against racial discrimination has essentially been won, but it remains a challenge for the black community to embrace the notion of civil responsibility. He states emphatically that "no people can be genuinely free so long as they look to others for their deliverance."[16] His vision of black progress is one of freedom, equality, and dignity, where the vicious cycle of poverty and dependency is brought to an end by the relentless pursuit of economic opportunity. Keeping in mind the goal of constructing a sense of self-worth, he separates the faults attributable to the oppressor from the responsibility that rests upon the shoulders of the oppressed:

> Neither the guilt nor the pity of one's oppressor is a sufficient basis upon which to construct a sense of self-worth. When faced with the ravages of black crime against blacks, the depressing nature of social life in many low-income black communities, the alarming incidence of pregnancy among unwed black teenagers, or the growing dependency of blacks on transfers from an increasingly hostile polity, it is simply insufficient to respond by saying "This is the fault of racist America. These problems will be solved when America finally does right by its black folk." Such a response dodges the issue of responsibility, both at the level of individual behavior (the criminal perpetrator being responsible for his act), and at the level of the group (the black community being responsible for the values embraced by its people).[17]

His argument for the separation of white fault from black responsibility notwithstanding, Loury attempts to apply a single standard to black and white social behavior based upon the assumption that there exists an objective relationship between effort and reward for individuals in the American society.

Cornel West has taught religion and Afro-American studies at Harvard, Princeton, and Union Theological Seminary. He published an article in *The Christian Century* in 1986 responding to Loury and other black conservatives, and continued the black liberal-conservative dialogue in his 1993 best-selling book, *Race Matters*. West's primary agenda in this debate has been to "unmask" and refute the ethical analyses and proposals of black conservatives. He offers a structural critique of black poverty that gives much greater weight to external factors than to internal ones, roughly in reverse proportion to Loury's greater emphasis upon internal factors in accounting for the economic predicament of blacks. There is one key difference, however, between Loury's attack on black liberals and West's counterattack on black conservatives. West concedes that "black liberalism indeed is inadequate, but argues that black conservativism is unacceptable."[18] Loury sees black liberalism as unacceptable, but makes no concessions with regard to the inadequacies and limitations of the black conservative position.

West understands the economic and political state of the black community that serves as a backdrop for the disarray of black liberalism and the emergence of black conservativism to include both structural and behavioral factors:

> The crisis of black liberalism and the emergence of the new black conservatives can best be understood in light of three fundamental events in American society and culture since 1973: the eclipse of U.S. economic and military predominance in the world; the structural transformation of the American economy; and the moral breakdown of communities throughout the country, especially among the black working poor and underclass.[19]

He observes that it is in the discussion of morality and behavior that black conservatives have had their most salutary effect on public discourse concerning the plight of African Americans, and he is quite willing to confront the conservatives' claim that the decline of values such as patience, hard work, deferred gratification, and self-reliance have resulted in the high crime rates, the increasing number of unwed mothers, and the relatively uncompetitive academic performances of black youth.[20] West is quick to point to external factors, however, to account for the negative patterns of behavior and social responsibility found among the black poor:

> Ought we to be surprised that black youths isolated from the labor market, marginalized by decrepit urban schools, devalued by alienating ideals of beauty and targeted by an unprecedented drug invasion exhibit high rates of crime and teen-age pregnancy?
>
> My aim is not to provide excuses for black behavior or to absolve blacks of personal responsibility. . . . We indeed must criticize and condemn immoral acts of black people, but we must do

so cognizant of the circumstances into which people are born and under which they live.[21]

West detects a consensus among black liberals and conservatives alike that moral regeneration is needed in poor black communities; in his view, however, neither group adequately speaks to this need. Furthermore, in his 1986 article West has no vision or prescription to offer for black progress. In a rather ambivalent statement, he suggests that while there are a few prophetic black churches that possess the kind of strategy that it takes to meet the cultural and moral crisis facing the black community, there are not enough of them. He even applauds the fact that by calling attention to the failures of black liberalism, black conservatives have encouraged blacks to entertain more progressive solutions to the problems of social injustice, but he does not indicate what these might be.

In *Race Matters* West reformulates the terms of the discussion of the plight of black America and produces a brief sketch of a progressive solution to the problem of social injustice. He begins by offering a more insightful and descriptive overview of black critical analyses of the plight of poor blacks in terms of two opposing camps:

> On the one hand, there are those who highlight the *structural* constraints on the life chances of black people. Their viewpoint involves a subtle historical and sociological analysis of slavery, Jim Crowism, job and residential discrimination, skewed unemployment rates, inadequate health care, and poor education. On the other hand, there are those who stress the *behavioral* impediments on black upward mobility. They focus on the waning of the Protestant ethic—hard work, deferred gratification, frugality, and responsibility—in much of black America.[22]

He designates the first group as liberal structuralists. Their prescription for black moral progress is based upon advocacy for full employment, health, education, and child-care programs, and broad affirmative action practices. He calls the second group conservative behaviorists, who would promote black moral progress by means of self-help programs, black business expansion, and nonpreferential job practices.[23]

One of the most important contributions West makes to the current understanding of the state of black America is the observation that the most basic issue now facing black America is nihilism, "the profound sense of psychological depression, personal worthlessness, and social despair so widespread in black America."[24] In his opinion, both liberals and conservatives alike have failed to grapple with the nihilistic threat to black existence in America, but the debate has engendered critical questions and perspectives that urge the formulation of some sort of political response.

West proposes a "politics of conversion" centered upon a love ethic and grounded in grassroots organizations whose leaders exemplify moral integrity, character, and democratic statesmanship. This politics of conversion resolves the liberal/conservative dilemma in a practical synthesis of divergent points of view:

> Like liberal structuralists, the advocates of a politics of conversion never lose sight of the structural conditions that shape the sufferings and lives of people. Yet, unlike liberal structuralism, the politics of conversion meets the nihilistic threat head-on. Like conservative behaviorism, the politics of conversion openly confronts the self-destructive and inhumane actions of black people. Unlike conservative behaviorists, the politics of conversion situates these actions within inhumane circumstances (but does not thereby exonerate them).[25]

Curiously, West does not name any of these advocates of a politics of conversion to give it concrete identity—it remains an abstraction. He cites Toni Morrison's novels to illustrate the love ethic, but offers no illustrations or examples of groups or organizations who are engaged in the task of promoting self-worth and self-affirmation in response to nihilism. For some reason, he has retreated from his earlier position of envisioning the prophetic black churches as the collective base of anti-nihilistic organization and activity.

Both West and Loury have honored the legacy of King in their work. In his *Prophetic Fragments,* West praises King as a prophetic Christian and as the most significant and successful "organic intellectual" in American history, borrowing Antonio Gramsci's term.[26] Foremost in West's assessment is King's voice and activity of protest. Although Loury is obviously less sanguine about black protest of any sort, he does acknowledge the ongoing importance of King's legacy of moral concern about the plight of poor blacks in America.

Ethics and God-Talk

The African American Christian thinkers brought under consideration here—David Walker, Maria Steward, Glenn Loury, and Cornel West—all point to similar facts of African American life, and all formulate the ethical issues in similar terms, that from the time of slavery to the present, the progress of blacks has been hindered by poverty and by the inability of blacks, for whatever reason, to exercise their full rights and responsibilities in American society. All agree that there are some fundamental moral norms that can be applied to measure the moral shortcomings of both the black community and the American society at large, although in the contemporary black conservative view the misconduct of blacks completely overshadows the sins of the society as a determinant of black progress.

But one of the most striking contrasts that emerges from this overview is the prevalence of God-talk in the two antebellum documents, and the total absence of any reference to God whatsoever by the two twentieth-century social critics. Walker and Steward begin and end with God-talk in their analyses of the problems and prospects of blacks in America. God is the ultimate source of their norms of personal morality and social responsibility, and the attributes of God convey an imperative for people to pursue justice, righteousness, and virtue in the world. Simply put, God defends the oppressed and judges the oppressor. Moreover, Walker and Steward derive their notions of human dignity, equality, and freedom from the belief that each human being reflects the image of God. So for the antebellum writers, God-talk is an indispensable element in both the external and internal dimensions of the black condition. White racism and oppression are condemned as sins against God, and for blacks, the self-help ethic is both an aspiration and an exhortation to fulfill one's own God-given potential. Clearly, for these Christians the voice of protest is an empowering prophetic utterance.

Is the omission of God-talk from the twentieth-century statements merely a reflection of the secularization of the present age? Has God-talk been discarded by modern intellectuals as a forgotten relic of a useless past? The absence of any reference to God is disturbing, given the historical ethical witness of the black churches, and especially in view of the fact that both Loury and West present cogent arguments that each other's prescriptions will not work. It seems that some appeal to the reality and power of God is sorely needed in view of the nihilistic emphasis of contemporary African American moral discourse, so that the search for prescriptions and the prospects for progress might be sustained beyond the limitations of inadequate social analyses and failed social policy.

Uplift

Toward the end of the nineteenth century, the cause of black empowerment and moral improvement was taken up by the black women's club movement. The motto of the National Association of Colored Women's Clubs, "Lifting as We Climb," is a succinct expression of the social ethical agenda of this movement, namely, the socioeconomic advancement, in solidarity with the oppressed and impoverished masses, of black women, men, and children. One of the early leaders, Fannie Barrier Williams, described the motive behind the motto:

> How to help and protect some defenseless and tempted young woman; how to aid some poor boy to complete a much-coveted education; how to lengthen the short school term in some impoverished school district; how to instruct deficient mothers in the difficulties of child training.[1]

The social ethical focus of this movement is further illuminated by Williams's explanation of the distinctive differences between black and white women's clubs in terms of purpose and social concern: "Among the colored women the club is the effort of the few competent in behalf of the many incompetent. . . . Among white women the club is the onward movement of the already uplifted."[2]

The motive that fueled this movement was not necessarily altruistic, because the educated and empowered elite black women understood that their fate was bound to the plight of the masses. Mary Church Terrell, one of the wealthiest and best-educated black women of her time, identified the empowerment of poor black women with the self-interest of the elite black women who were also victimized by the society's overt biases based on race and sex: "Self-preservation demands that [black women] go among the lowly, illiterate and even the vicious, to whom they are bound by ties of race and sex . . . to reclaim them."[3] Notwithstanding the forced solidarity brought to bear upon these women by racism and sexism, the intention to "reclaim" the lowly represents an important African American tradition of social and spiritual empowerment.

Club Women, Church Women, and Black Liberation

To be sure, the empowerment ethics of the black women's club movement of the late nineteenth and early twentieth centuries has become the focus of a number of recent monographs in black theology and ethics.[4] In her book *Awake, Arise and Act*, womanist ethicist Marcia Riggs retrieves three elements from the moral vision of the nineteenth-century black club women, which she commends as a guide to the socioeconomic praxis of black liberation: renunciation, inclusivity, and responsibility. *Renunciation* means the willingness on the part of the black female elite to give up the "privilege of difference" in order to work with other classes of women. *Inclusivity* is the removal of boundaries and the respecting of difference as the necessary point of departure for understanding and actualizing authentic unity, as stated in the September 1897 minutes of the National Association of Colored Women: "by the help of God to secure harmony of action and cooperation among all women in raising to the highest plane, home, moral and civil life."[5] Following H. Richard Niebuhr's social ethics as developed in *The Responsible Self,* Riggs understands *responsibility* as "fitting" responses that mediate the fulfillment of the obligation and duty to racial uplift with the belief in God's justice for all people:

> The black club women undertook their social reform efforts in terms of what they understood as the intrinsic connection between work on behalf of black women and all black people (the particular) and the greater good, reform of society aimed at justice for all (the universal).[6]

The institutional embodiment of Christian ethics and empowerment in the lives and work of African American women not only occurred within the club movement but also in the churches. Typically, these club women were also lay leaders in their churches. In her book *Righteous Discontent,* historian Evelyn Brooks Higginbotham describes the work of empowered black church women who embodied ethical principles of freedom and justice: "largely through the fund-raising efforts of women, the black church built schools, provided clothes and food to poor people, established old folks' homes and orphanages, and made available a host of needed social welfare services." She sees her study as an attempt to "rescue women from invisibility as historical actors in the drama of black empowerment." In her view, their efforts represented "everyday forms of resistance to oppression and demoralization."[7] Higginbotham argues convincingly that women were crucial to broadening the public arm of the church and making it the most powerful institution of racial self-help in the African American community.

Higginbotham identifies a "politics of respectability" in the black Baptist women's movement. Insisting upon black conformity to white norms of manners and morals, the politics of respectability emphasized reform of individual behavior "both as a goal in itself and as a strategy for reform of the entire structural system of American race relations."[8] These women condemned white racism, but were also critical of the negative practices and attitudes of black people. The politics of respectability did not reduce to an accommodationist stance toward racism, or a compensatory ideology in the face of powerlessness:

> Through the discourse of respectability, the Baptist women emphasized manners and morals while simultaneously asserting traditional forms of protest, such as petitions, boycotts, and verbal appeals to justice. Ultimately, the rhetoric of the Woman's Convention combined both a conservative and a radical impulse.[9]

In a similar vein, social ethicist Theodore Walker addresses the radical and conservative aspects of the black church women's movement in relation to the later development of black power:

> It is true that these women were more likely to have spoken of "uplift" rather than "empowerment." Nonetheless, their moral commitment to the idea that black women, black people, and black churches should exercise their powers of education and socialization in ways that improve the circumstances of black homes, families, and tribes here and abroad places their social ethical thought unequivocally within the category of social ethical thinking we now call the philosophy of black power.[10]

The leaders of these clubs and church organizations rose to prominence precisely because they articulated openly and eloquently the yearning and indignation of the masses, and "captured their people's vision of America—a vision that was simultaneously optimistic and critical, but ultimately hopeful."[11]

To illustrate in further detail the empowerment ethics undergirding the task of uplift, a closer examination is offered of the lives of two outstanding individuals who embodied the ideals of the black church women's movement and the black women's club movement, respectively: Nannie Helen Burroughs and Mary McLeod Bethune.

Nannie Helen Burroughs

Nannie Helen Burroughs (1878–1961) was an educator, colum-
nist, and religious leader. In 1901 she became the first corresponding secretary of the Women's Auxiliary of the National
Baptist Convention, and in 1948 she was elected president of the
National Baptist Women's Convention. Throughout her life she
traveled extensively giving speeches advocating the cause of black
women, and during the 1920s and 1930s she wrote a column
for the *Pittsburgh Courier.* A report acknowledging Burroughs's
charismatic leadership and outstanding speaking ability was
published in the June 28, 1903 edition of the *National Baptist
Union,* the weekly newspaper of the National Baptist Convention:

> Miss N. H. Burroughs appeared before the Convention for the
> first time, and like Saul, towered head and shoulders above the
> men in Israel for the magnetism of her speech, the earnestness of
> her appeal, the nobleness of her work, all of which combined
> called for such an ovation that has not been given in the annals of
> our "Distinctive Baptist" work. When she finished speaking tears
> flowed from some; applause was deafening from others; while
> young and old, white and black, cast money at her feet with an
> enthusiasm that has never been equaled in the history of our Con-
> vention.[12]

Although Higginbotham argues forcefully for the importance of
Baptist lay women's work over against the relative insignificance
of women ministers in the history of the black church, Burroughs
and others obviously exercised great preaching ability, and were
capable of raising sizeable offerings, whether properly ordained
or not.[13] Her speeches and writings convey her forthright manner
in addressing the issues with a critical perspective. The following
excerpt from an address entitled "What Must the Negro Do to
Be Saved?" delivered to a young people's forum at Bethel African
Methodist Episcopal Church in 1933 clearly expresses her social

ethics and her commitment to the empowerment of black people, as well as her penchant for sarcasm:

> Chloroform your "Uncle Toms." The Negro must unload the leeches and parasitic leaders who are absolutely eating the life out of the struggling, desiring mass of people. . . . I like that quotation, "Moses, my servant, is dead. Therefore, arise and go over Jordan." There are no deliverers. They're all dead. We must arise and go over Jordan. We can take the promised land.
>
> The Negro must serve notice on the world that he is ready to die for justice. To struggle and battle and overcome and absolutely defeat every force designed against us is the only way to achieve. More than this, the Negro must glorify the things of the spirit and keep the things of the flesh under control. We must get a correct sense of values.[14]

One of Burroughs's lasting contributions to the religious life of African American women was her initiation of the observance of "Woman's Day" in the Baptist churches. These churches generally did not endorse women preachers. The idea was first implemented in July 1907 with the purpose of encouraging women to raise funds for foreign missions, and, in the process, to develop public speakers among the ranks of church women: "besides raising money for Foreign Missions, 'Woman's Day' was intended to raise the women themselves—training them for public speaking and informed leadership through authentic, prepared, challenging speeches—music and techniques on how to get, willingly, larger contributions for Foreign Missions."[15] Years later Burroughs lamented that her idea had been co-opted by male and female church leaders to raise funds for local congregations and pastors rather than for missions:

> Because of the way the purpose of WOMAN'S DAY has been diverted, our churches are reaping a financial harvest for church buildings, improvements and every conceivable local benefit. The promoters send off each year to get a WOMAN'S DAY speaker. Somebody who can draw a crowd. Had the original plan been followed, the churches would now have well-prepared speakers of

their own. WOMAN'S DAY would be a real educational and spiritual achievement, blessing the local churches beyond imagination. . . . "Woman's Day," properly used, would put women's feet in the path of service and lift their heads up to see the field ripe unto harvest. But instead, women prance up and down church aisles, passing envelopes and baskets begging for money to beat the men.[16]

Her main disappointment was that once these annual Woman's Day celebrations had been co-opted by the male-dominated churches, the purpose shifted to raising money rather than elevating women.

Nevertheless, Burroughs remained totally committed to the spiritual, educational, economic, and political development of black women and their families. In 1909 she founded the National Training School for Women and Girls in Washington, D. C., whose fundamental educational philosophy was based on the motto, "Bible, bath, and broom." One of the school's key educational objectives was to professionalize domestic work (one of the few areas of employment open to black women at the time) so that more black women could be gainfully employed to support themselves and their families. Burroughs also organized the National Association of Wage Earners during the 1920s to attract public attention to the plight of black working women.

Burroughs waged her struggle against prejudice and discrimination on moral terms, constantly chastising her race for overindulgence in the material aspects of life. She tried to teach black people that the preoccupation with wealth and luxury was endemic to white society, and would eventually mark its doom. She promoted racial unity and collective struggle. Although she renounced individualism, she was unwilling to substitute individual examples of achievement for the realization of group advancement. She encouraged blacks to use "ballots and dollars" to fight racism instead of "wasting time begging the white race for mercy." Her understanding of Christian ethics did not allow for toleration of abuse by whites: "It is no evidence of Christianity to have people mock you and spit on you and defeat the future of your children. It is a mark of cowardice."[17] Burroughs's embodied advocacy of empowerment ethics remains worthy of emulation by leaders in today's black churches.

Mary McLeod Bethune

Mary McLeod Bethune, a contemporary of Burroughs who lived from 1875 to 1955, arose from abject poverty as the child of former slaves in rural South Carolina to become the leading black female educator, clubwoman, and political power broker of her time. She was the fifteenth of seventeen children born to the McLeod family, and she was chosen to go to school in order that she could teach her siblings at home. From the age of twelve she desired to become a missionary to Africa, and she went to Moody Bible Institute in Chicago to pursue the necessary training for this work. The Presbyterian Board of Missions, however, rejected her application for appointment to a missionary station in Africa. After serving in several teaching positions, in 1904 she founded the Daytona Normal and Industrial School for Negro Girls in Daytona Beach, Florida, with no funds or sponsors. This institution later merged with Cookman Institute in Florida to create a coeducational school under the sponsorship of the Methodist Episcopal Board of Education. In 1923 Bethune became president of the Bethune-Cookman Institute, left the Presbyterian Church, and became a Methodist. In 1935 she founded the National Council of Negro Women (NCNW), a federation of national women's organizations that united the masses of black women in America, lobbied on behalf of their concerns in various national and international settings, and forged alliances with white women's groups. During the 1930s she was appointed by President Franklin Delano Roosevelt to serve as Director of the Negro Division of the National Youth Administration, with responsibility for finding employment for young people between the ages of 16 and 24 in private industry, work relief, and vocational training projects. She was a close friend of Eleanor Roosevelt, and used this friendship politically to direct attention to black women's concerns. She enjoyed high visibility as a member of Roosevelt's "Black Cabinet."

Bethune was known for her regal bearing and spellbinding oratory. Her religious upbringing, strong sense of identity with the poor, and pride in her African heritage would serve her well in the work of education for black empowerment. Her sense of mission in this regard was influenced by her distinctively positive attitude toward Africa; she often expressed pride that "pure African blood" flowed in her veins and that her mother had come from a matriarchal tribe and royal African ancestry.[18] A statue of Bethune stands in one of the public parks in the city of Washington, the only such national monument ever erected in honor of a black woman.

The minutes of a NCNW meeting describe a conference Bethune convened at the White House in 1938 to involve black women in the formulation of public policy on a national level:

> Sixty-seven Negro women marching to the White House in their own right, standing on their feet expressing what they thought concerning their own people and the participation they should have had in the general affairs of the country. . . . I was glad to sit aside them and see them stand on their feet fearlessly preparing themselves and their thoughts, not coming as beggars but coming as women wanting to participate in the administration of a human problem.[19]

As a protest leader, Bethune was adamant about the unheralded achievements of women, and always encouraged them to "go to the front and take our rightful place; fight our battles and claim our victories."[20] Clarence G. Newsome has written a thoughtful commentary on the relationship between Bethune's religious faith and style of leadership:

> Mary Bethune's religious faith fostered a style of leadership characterized on one hand by a charismatic personality and a spirit of

protest, and on the other, by a pragmatic disposition and the politics of compromise. Her charisma emanated primarily from an overwhelming confidence that providence was active in her personal history. Her pragmatism resulted largely from confrontation with the social realities of racism, sexism and poverty.[21]

In keeping with what Riggs has said about the ethics of the black women's club movement in general, Bethune embraced not only the cause of racial equality, but also the larger cause of human justice. Her active commitment to social change was fueled by her zealous embrace of evangelical Christianity, although her Christian witness was most often expressed outside the context of the institutional church.

Shortly before her death in 1955, Bethune published a statement that was broadly circulated in *Ebony* magazine as a virtual manifesto of black empowerment ethics. "My Last Will and Testament" exhorts Negroes to embrace several principles and virtues in order to establish racial equality and freedom—love, hope, thirst for education, faith, racial dignity, brotherhood, and a responsibility to young people—each listed with insights drawn from her own experience.

I LEAVE YOU LOVE. . . . Our aim must be to create a world of fellowship and justice where no man's color or religion is held against him.

I LEAVE YOU HOPE. Yesterday, our ancestors endured the degradation of slavery, yet they retained their dignity. Today, we direct our economic and political strength toward winning a more abundant and secure life. Tomorrow, a new Negro, unhindered by race taboos and shackles, will benefit from this striving and struggling.

I LEAVE YOU A THIRST FOR EDUCATION. More and more, Negroes are taking full advantage of hard-won opportunities for learning, and the educational level of the Negro population is at its highest point in history.

I LEAVE YOU FAITH. . . . The measure of our progress as a

race is in precise relation to the depth of our faith in our people held by our leaders.

I LEAVE YOU RACIAL DIGNITY. . . . We, as Negroes, must recognize that we are the custodians as well as the heirs of a great civilization.

I LEAVE YOU A DESIRE TO LIVE HARMONIOUSLY WITH YOUR FELLOW MEN. The problem of color is world wide, on every continent. I appeal to all to recognize their common problems, and unite to solve them.

I LEAVE YOU FINALLY A RESPONSIBILITY TO OUR YOUNG PEOPLE. . . . We have a powerful potential in our youth, and we must have the courage to change old ideas and practices so that we may direct their power toward good ends.[22]

Bethune's exhortation to universal love, her appreciation of the hope and dignity of struggle, her view of education as a means of achieving personal ambition, her insistence upon a positive sense of black identity and historical awareness, her global consciousness of the reality of racism, and her optimism with regard to the next generation, all testify to the engagement of black women in the pursuit of justice for all people.

Bethune's leadership legacy has been carried forth with distinction for many years by NCNW President Dorothy Height. One of the most widely publicized initiatives undertaken by the NCNW in recent years is a national Black Family Reunion Celebration, convened annually in Washington, D. C., which uses corporate sponsorships to provide information, entertainment, and cultural enrichment for families.

Both Bethune and Burroughs exemplify a noteworthy tradition of Christian social activism. Their calling was to a life of commitment to the educational and cultural development of black women, as expressed in their professional work as educators and in their leadership in religious and political organizations concerned with the plight of black women. Although Burroughs was more overtly critical in her speeches than Bethune, each in her own way framed the problems of racism, sexism, and poverty in ethical terms, giving special attention to the role of moral wisdom in the progress of black people. Neither woman mothered daughters in the biological sense, but both gave priority to the needs of young black women, on whose behalf they worked creatively to formulate and communicate systems of ethical understanding designed to promote individual and collective growth. Their commitment to uplift, empowered by a bold vision of the imperative to love God, neighbor, and self, inspired countless black women to become engaged in a dynamic movement toward justice and human wholeness through their churches and clubs.

Uplift and Empowerment in the Holiness Churches

The Holiness churches came to prominence during the same historical period as the emergence of black women's clubs and the women's movement in the black Baptist churches. What is significant about these churches in the early years is their openness to women's leadership and ordination to ministry. Perhaps the most important reason for early acceptance of women's leadership in the Holiness churches is the simple fact that the nineteenth-century Holiness revival that gave birth to these churches was centered upon the contributions of a white Methodist laywoman, Phoebe Palmer (1807–1874). She is often referred to as the "Mother of the Holiness Movement." The revival was engendered by the "Tuesday Meeting for the Promotion of Holiness," which began in Palmer's home and continued for some sixty years, even beyond the time of her death. In 1859 Palmer wrote a defense of women's right to preach: "She argued from the promise of Joel 2:28, reiterated by Peter at Pentecost in Acts 2:17-18, that God the Father has promised that in the latter days the Holy Spirit will be given to women as well as to men, and that both will be expected and compelled to pray, prophesy and preach."[23] The Holiness movement affirmed the leadership of women because of its teaching that the Holy Spirit gives gifts of ministry and ecclesiastical authority in the church without regard to race, sex, or class. Another factor that helps to explain the acceptance of women's ministry by Holiness groups was the requirement that all persons publicly testify to their experience of conversion and sanctification as a second work of grace, which served as an open invitation for women to have a significant voice in the church.[24]

The practical dimension of Phoebe Palmer's ministry included the Hedding Church, a city mission work predating the urban settlement houses; service as an officer of the New York Assistance Society for the Relief and Religious Instruction of the Sick Poor; and the Five Points Mission, which housed and provided schooling for some twenty poor families in New York.[25] Following Palmer's lead, it became characteristic of Holiness women to establish empowering ministries among the poor and the homeless in the cities. Mary Cole, a pioneering evangelist in the Church of God (Anderson, Indiana), moved to Chicago in 1898 to assume responsibility for a rescue mission that offered food and lodging to homeless men. Another Church of God evangelist, Nora Hunter, assisted the homeless in Los Angeles in locating housing and helped newcomers find jobs and food.[26]

Women's empowerment was a factor in the early history of the Church of the Nazarene, which came into existence toward the end of the nineteenth century under the influence of the Holiness revival. Women were primarily responsible for starting the church's missionary work, its youth work, and its first educational institution, the Pacific Bible School.[27] As early as 1905, presumably in response to rising opposition to women ministers, Fannie MacDowell Hunter published the book *Women Preachers*, containing the stories of twelve women who insisted "that they had been 'called' to ministry—first to foreign missions (where women were welcome), but that God had providentially led them into home missions and then pastoral work."[28]

The Salvation Army is perhaps the best-known example of a Christian denomination that gave priority to the empowerment of women and the poor around the turn of the century. Most people in the United States today know the Salvation Army only as a charitable organization that uses bells and kettles to solicit contributions from Christmas shoppers outside department stores, and sells donated items at greatly reduced prices at its chain of outlet stores. The Salvation Army, however, is an international denomination in the Wesleyan-Holiness tradition, with headquarters in England. Co-founder Catherine Booth (1829–1890) worked in close partnership with her husband William as a preacher and urban missionary whose special ministry in London's West End was to reclaim women from a life of prostitution.[29]

Norris Magnuson's *Salvation in the Slums: Evangelical Social Work, 1865–1920* documents the involvement of the Salvation Army in the "gospel welfare movement," whose openness toward and identification with the poor was based on continuing close personal contacts and settlement houses whose workers literally became "neighbors of the poor." Because participants in the gospel welfare movement centered their faith in the ethical principle of love, rather than in a doctrinal creed, their constant practical emphasis helped them keep that principle from evaporating into sentimentality: "The right kind of religion is love with its coat off, doing its best to help somebody."[30] The love ethic empowered this movement to embrace blacks as worthy and capable persons, in contrast to the neglect of blacks, Asians, and other classes by the more "progressive" social gospel movement: "In a day when the plight of blacks was worsening, the Salvation Army and kindred organizations defended them and welcomed them into rescue institutions for assistance and as fellow-workers."[31] Moreover, the Salvation Army leadership fully understood the poverty they encountered in its social, political, and economic context:

"We must have justice—more justice," the *New York Tribune* quoted Ballington Booth, commander of the American Salvation

Army forces, as saying. "To right the social wrong by charity," he had said, "is like bailing the ocean with a thimble . . . We must readjust our social machinery so that the producers of wealth become also owners of wealth."[32]

Thus the empowerment ethics promoted by the Salvation Army included a deep concern for economic justice.

In general, the Holiness movement attracted significant numbers of blacks beginning in the late nineteenth century. Black Holiness women employed as domestic workers in the city of Los Angeles comprised the core group of the Azusa Street Revival from which the Pentecostal movement emerged in 1906 under the leadership of William J. Seymour. In Seymour's own words, "The work began among the colored people. God baptized several sanctified wash women with the Holy Ghost, who have been much used of Him."[33] The Pentecostal movement emphasized the spiritual empowerment of men, women, and children of all races and social classes, as manifested by the practice of speaking in tongues, in accordance with the Pentecost experienced by the men and women of the early church (Acts 2:1-18). A number of Baptist and Methodist women came over into the black Holiness and Pentecostal churches where women were given authority to exercise their gifts.[34]

The focus upon uplift and empowerment eventually waned among the Holiness churches, as the adherence to the Holiness ethic of moral purity became identified with the characteristically American quest for status and upward mobility, and the move to the suburbs came to signify the realization of spiritual and worldly success. Concomitant with the flight of Holiness people and their churches to the suburbs was the effective abandonment of moral and spiritual responsibility for compassionate ministry to the urban poor. Furthermore, being located in the suburbs made it easier to justify exclusion of blacks, who, given the firmly entrenched patterns of segregation in housing throughout this century, generally have not lived or worshiped in suburban areas.

As the Holiness churches tended to become more closely identified ethically, theologically, and demographically with mainline Protestantism, they fell in line with the mainstream's discrimination against blacks and other minorities, rejection of women's leadership, and disregard of the concerns of the poor. It can be assumed, then, that as racism, sexism, and class consciousness increased in the Holiness churches, the acceptance of women's leadership and the commitment to ministries of uplift declined. To some extent the black Holiness churches have deviated from this pattern, insofar as they have remained in the urban areas, and maintained a sense of identity with the poor and other victims of discrimination. In his landmark study of Pentecostalism in America, historian Robert Mapes Anderson notes that by the end of World War I, "the inner-city, store-front mission phase of the Holiness movement was passing rapidly and the middle-class propensities of Holiness believers were unmistakable."[35] As the religion of Holiness believers became a positive asset in achieving upward mobility, they tended to relinquish their sense of solidarity with and social ethical concern for the poor.

Christian Ethics and the Crisis of the Poor

Empowerment of the poor remains an especially difficult task in a racist and sexist society where the most vulnerable persons are nonwhite single women and their fatherless children. The majority of black children who live in households headed by single women live in poverty, and a significant proportion of all black children live in families with incomes below the poverty line.

The Bible contains repeated warnings of God's judgment against those who oppress widows and orphans, often in conjunction with admonitions not to oppress the stranger—that is, not to be racist. Among the most dramatic healing narratives in the Gospels are those that feature Jesus responding to the desperate need of women who are alone, such as the raising of the only son of the widow of Nain from his funeral bier, and the healing of the demon-possessed daughter of the Canaanite woman who challenges Jesus to share the "children's bread" not only with the lost sheep of the house of Israel, but also with the Gentile world. In the New Testament epistle of James, pure and undefiled religion is defined in terms of two activities: "to care for orphans and widows in their distress, and to keep oneself unstained from the world." (James 1:27) This biblical mandate speaks directly to Christians who seek to promote empowerment ethics and compassionate ministries in the context of holy living, especially among those widowed and made fatherless by death, as well as those who have been bereft of husbands and fathers as a consequence of divorce, drug addiction, and the society's drift toward wholesale devaluation of the covenants of marriage and family.

The American society has become well-acclimated in recent years to the female-headed household as the normative family structure in the black community, but the crisis of the 1990s seems to be total family breakdown, where even mothers and grandmothers are abandoning family responsibilities, primarily due to the abuse of crack, cocaine, and alcohol. In addition, the spread of Acquired Immune Deficiency Syndrome (AIDS) among black and Hispanic women and their newborn infants is alarming in its proportions. Many inner-city hospitals are faced with growing numbers of "boarder babies," newborns whose biological mothers have left them to die if they have AIDS, or, if they are healthy enough to survive, to live indefinitely in hospital nurseries until placed with adoptive or foster parents. These factors, combined with the problems of poverty, teenage pregnancy, violent crime, unemployment, and homelessness, create a severe drain upon all the institutional resources society has devised to meet human need, including families, welfare agencies, private charities, hospitals, and churches.

Writing in *Christianity and Crisis,* political scientist Jerry G. Watts has framed the problem of poverty in the United States in moral terms:

The crisis of the poor in the United States lies in one fact: The resources needed to end poverty are readily available, but the will to end poverty is non-existent. . . . On present evidence, then, it is not at all clear that our society has the moral integrity to end poverty. Regardless of the ease, cost-effectiveness, or self-interest involved in generating a more humane society, until we begin to care, to develop communal articulations of empathy, all our planning will be in vain. Until then, the poor will continue to be destroyed—and with them, most remnants of our claim to humanity.[36]

The record shows that the black women who organized themselves in the clubs and the churches to do the work of uplift, and their sisters in the Holiness movement, embodied the same empowerment ethics they sought to instill in the oppressed women, men, and children of their communities. Although the theme of "lifting as we climb" has been discarded as outmoded and obsolete based upon present-day social views and moral sensitivities, it still points effectively to the crux of the dilemma that hinders the engagement of affluent Christians with the poor today, namely, Why should those who have been empowered to "climb" be concerned to "lift" those who languish in poverty and degradation? Christian women such as Nannie Helen Burroughs, Mary McLeod Bethune, Phoebe Palmer, Catherine Booth, Mary Cole, Nora Hunter, and many others responded to this dilemma by committing themselves to "climb" and "lift" by means of sermons, speeches, and the establishment of missionary societies and schools. Indeed, these women exemplify the moral integrity and communal articulations of empathy that will be required for the development and extension of ministries of uplift and empowerment for America's poor in the twenty-first century.

Cooperation

The church has been the foremost arena for the empowerment of African American people throughout most of their sojourn in North America. Occasionally this empowerment has been experienced as full cooperation between the sexes, in which both men and women have worked together toward a common purpose. Patterns of sexism and discrimination in many black churches persist, however, where men have established structures, precedents, and hermeneutics (often with the support of women) to exclude women from empowerment for leadership.[1] While contemporary black religious scholars are now directing critical attention toward this problem with reference to the black churches in general, inadequate attention has been given to those Holiness and Pentecostal religious bodies that historically promoted egalitarian ecclesial practices and biblical hermeneutics.

Holiness and Pentecostal Church History: Race, Sex, and Class

In their revisionist critique of American church historiography, *The Churching of America, 1776–1990: Winners and Losers in*

Our Religious Economy, Roger Finke and Rodney Stark carefully analyze this oversight among mainstream church historians. They note that, at worst, the Holiness churches have been consigned to historical insignificance because they are regarded as losers, as "misguided conservatives expelled from the mainline bodies," and as "unsophisticated souls, sadly out of joint with modern times." However, they argue forcefully that church historians should give full recognition to the impact of these churches based on the numbers:

> Any fair history based on the subsequent fate of religious organizations would have to acknowledge that the Holiness Movement gave birth to denominations that have been growing rapidly, while the denominations that drove out the Holiness Movement have been rapidly losing out ever since.[2]

The most impressive example of this observation is the Church of God in Christ, a black Pentecostal denomination with roots in the Holiness movement. Some 3.7 million members strong, this group has surpassed several of the mainline Protestant churches in total membership, including the Presbyterian Church, U.S.A. (2.9 million), the Episcopal Church (2.4 million), the United Church of Christ (1.7 million), and the American Baptist Churches in the U.S.A. (1.6 million).[3]

Donald Dayton has also addressed the historiographical biases against the Holiness movement, supporting his argument with several interesting comparisons:

> On a given Sunday there are as many holiness folk in church as Methodists. To move on to other comparisons, there are as many folk in holiness churches on a given Sunday as there are members of Presbyterian churches in the USA. There are about as many members of holiness churches as there are Anglicans in the USA.[4]

Dayton declares that his study of the history of the ministry of women forced him to rethink the whole range of historiographical questions with respect to the Holiness movement.[5] Sociologist Cheryl Townsend Gilkes notes the tendency among both black and white sociologists who have studied organizations and structures within urban ghetto communities to ignore small churches pastored by women precisely *because* they were pastored by women.[6]

By the turn of the century, the ordination of women was accepted virtually throughout the Holiness movement. And when Pentecostalism emerged shortly thereafter, "it carried through this theme and was perhaps even more consistent in the practice of the ministry and ordination of women."[7] Compared to mainline denominations that began ordaining women only in recent years, the Holiness movement has a "usable past."[8] Women in five Wesleyan-Holiness denominations—Church of God (Anderson, Indiana), Church of the Nazarene, Free Methodist Church, Salvation Army, and the Wesleyan Church—currently constitute twenty-five percent of the clergy in their denominations, whereas women comprise only seven percent of the clergy in thirty-nine other denominations that now ordain women.[9]

Over the course of the twentieth century, however, there has been a dramatic and substantial decline in women's ecclesial leadership in the Holiness and Pentecostal churches. Church historian Susie Stanley cites statistics showing that the proportion of women clergy in the Church of the Nazarene fell precipitously from twenty percent in 1908 to one percent more recently, and, in the Church of God (Anderson, Indiana), from thirty-two percent in 1925 to fifteen percent. Other churches in the Wesleyan-Holiness tradition that ordain women show similar patterns of decline, with the sole exception of the Salvation Army, where women today still constitute a majority of commissioned officers, or ministers, as they did a century ago in 1896.[10] As early as 1939, a Church of God publication set forth a radical theological and ethical commentary upon the decline of women preachers:

> The prevalence of women preachers is a fair measure of the spirituality of a church, a country, or an age. As the church grows more

apostolic and more deeply spiritual, women preachers and workers abound in that church; as it grows more worldly and cold, the ministry of women is despised and gradually ceases altogether. It is of the nature of paganism to hate foreign people and to despise women, but the spirit of the gospel is exactly opposite.[11]

In this view, the rejection of women's ministerial leadership represents a worldly loss of focus upon the egalitarian spirit of the Christian gospel. Not surprisingly, the reestablishment of barriers to church leadership by most of the Holiness-Pentecostal groups on the basis of sex in the early decades of this century coincided with their increased complicity with prevailing mainstream practices of racial separation and segregation.

On the whole, the Holiness-Pentecostal movement in the United States has made a distinctive contribution to the historical evolution of religion in America by involving blacks, women, and the poor at all levels of ministry. There are well over a hundred church bodies listed in the *Directory of African American Religious Bodies* that can be identified as Holiness or Pentecostal. These churches were led by black Christians around the turn of the century who "came out" of the black Baptist and Methodist churches, seeking "the deeper life of entire sanctification" and Spirit baptism: "Their initial concern was not so much to start a new denomination as to call the existing ones back to the wells of their spirituality."[12] What the Holiness and Pentecostal churches have in common is an emphasis upon the experience of Spirit baptism. A crucial point of disagreement among them, however, is whether or not a person must speak with tongues (*glossolalia*) to validate his or her Spirit baptism. Pentecostals generally affirm the necessity of speaking in tongues. Some Holiness believers reject *glossolalia* altogether, while others appreciate and/or practice speaking in tongues without insisting upon the doctrine of tongues. Historically, these churches have been known to preach and promote an ascetic ethic forbidding the use of alcohol, tobacco, and other addictive substances, gambling, and secular dancing. They are sometimes called "Sanctified" churches because they all adhere to some form of doctrine and practice of sanctification.

Although some of these churches have adopted the sexist and racist norms of white mainline Protestantism, others have produced compelling models of empowerment by cooperation between men and women. Three distinct models of male-female cooperation—egalitarian, charismatic, and dialectical—will be illustrated here using cases taken from the Sanctified church tradition.

Egalitarian Cooperation in the Church of God

Although the Church of God (Anderson, Indiana) in the U.S.A. is relatively small, with 221,346 members in 2,295 congregations, the observation that as many as twenty percent of its congregations and fifteen percent of its membership are black sets it apart from the dominant American pattern of ecclesial racial separation.[13] Moreover, in recent years black ministers have occupied several major leadership positions within the group, including chief executive officer, president of the governing assembly of ministers, and dean of the graduate theological seminary at Anderson. Almost all of the black ministers and congregations are affiliates of an organization known as the National Association of the Church of God. The National Association is not a separate denomination and does not grant ministerial credentials, but does have its own administrative structures, physical plant, conventions, and educational ministries.

As early as 1917, at about the same time when other Holiness and Pentecostal bodies were resolving the race dilemma by splitting along racial lines, blacks in the Church of God established their own annual camp meeting in West Middlesex, Pennsylvania, near the Ohio state line. The core group that started this camp meeting association included Elisha and Priscilla Wimbish, a black Baptist couple from Cleveland. In 1904 Brother Wimbish had a vision of a camp meeting site, as told by his wife Priscilla:

"crowds and crowds of real happy people having church out in the woods where there were beautiful buildings among the trees . . . every time he had a chance to go to the woods he would look for the place."[14] Brother Wimbish's nephew Jerry Luck recalls his uncle's repeated testimony of the details of his vision of "a very large place on a hill and the people of God gathering from far and near to worship God in Spirit and truth. He also saw a part was lower farm land with a large house to shelter the saints in time of famine and there was a cemetery to bury the old and poor saints as they pass on from labor to reward."[15] The Wimbishes moved to Sharon, Pennsylvania and joined a Baptist church there, all the while still searching for the site he had seen in the vision.

Sister Wimbish sought permission from her Baptist pastor to organize a prayer band that met on Friday evenings and Sunday mornings after service to promote love and forgiveness, prompted by her concern for the hatred that existed among the members. These gatherings led Sister Wimbish and her followers to the experience of Spirit baptism and sanctification:

> By much prayer and fasting and studying the scriptures Sister Wimbish was baptized with the Holy Spirit and taught it to us, as a second definite experience which sanctifies all who receive Him and gives us power to live a clean holy life, without which no man can see the Lord.[16]

For some reason, the men in the prayer band were expelled from the Baptist church, but not the women. In her own testimony of the group's origins, Sister Wimbish clearly states that she left of her own accord, following what she perceived to be the voice of God:

> We saw the need of a closer walk with God so we started a little prayer band and called it, "The Brothers and Sisters of Love." Those who wanted more of God in their lives became members of the prayer band. We earnestly prayed and studied our Bibles. God revealed the light of His word to us, saved and sanctified us.

God spoke to me later and said, "Come out." I did not know what the voice meant but I obeyed and came out with about seven who followed me. We continued our services in homes and on the streets.[17]

Unhindered by the actions the Baptist church took against her followers, Sister Wimbish took her prayer band ministry door-to-door and to the streets of Sharon, Pennsylvania. This group of black saints sensed that they were being led by God and invested with divine authority to do ministry among the people.

The Brothers and Sisters of Love received guidance from both white and black ministers during this period. Grant Anderson, a white Church of God minister, invited the black saints to join the nearby Emlenton Church of God camp meeting instead of starting their own camp meeting. Brother Anderson also introduced the group to R. J. Smith, a black minister who had just moved from Freeport, New York to pastor a Church of God congregation in Pittsburgh. The black saints accepted Brother Anderson's encouragement to become a part of the Church of God.[18]

In 1912 the Lord sent some Church of God ministers to us, Brother J. L. Williams, J. G. Anderson, R. J. Smith and Brother and Sister Pye. It was through these ministers we received light on the church and changed our name from the Brothers and Sisters of Love to the Church of God.[19]

Their depth of conviction concerning acceptance of egalitarian spiritual leadership without regard to race or sex is revealed by this recollection of how the Brothers and Sisters of Love became affiliated with the Church of God. The five ministers who appealed to them are not identified by race, but simply as men and women sent by God.

The egalitarian custom of referring to the saints as "Brother" and "Sister," without regard to whether or not they are ordained clergy or pastors, was not peculiar to the Brothers and Sisters of Love prayer band, but was and is widely practiced within the Church of God, and especially in the black congregations. In a pattern often repeated in the formation of black churches in the Sanctified movement, the fledgling group was led and housed by women, and once the congregation was established, a man was called as pastor.

After the Church of God congregation was established in Sharon, Brother Wimbish persisted in seeking the fulfillment of his vision for a campground for the saints. Brother Smith, who had become a spiritual advisor to the congregation, "caught the vision" and began looking for a campsite in the Pittsburgh area. The site was found by Brother J. A. Christman. While hunting in the woods of West Middlesex, he came upon a hill that reminded him of the place Brother Wimbish had often mentioned in his testimonies. When taken to the site by Brother Christman, he confirmed that indeed it was the place he had seen in his dreams.[20]

The saints purchased 127 acres of land, and in August 1917 held their first camp meeting. Men and women worked together in constructing the camp meeting facilities and in leading worship. One woman in particular showed a remarkable range of abilities in this regard; Sister Nelson of Pittsburgh cut trees with the men, helped to install windows, door frames, and roofing, and prayed the first prayer in the first camp meeting![21]

The egalitarian cooperative empowerment of these men and women effected their resolve to maintain an open, interracial fellowship at the West Middlesex camp meeting. Prior to 1915, blacks had been attending the international camp meeting convened at Anderson, Indiana, a predominantly white gathering, for a number of years. Black ministers such as Abraham Stroud of Alabama and evangelist J. D. Smoot had been featured as camp meeting speakers. The Church of God General Assembly, a governing body of ministers that is convened each year at the Anderson meeting, passed a resolution in 1915 to form separate congregations, "so that the whites may win more whites and the blacks may win more blacks."[22] Mother Laura Moore, an early convert to the Brothers and Sisters of Love along with her husband Samuel, gives an account of her experience at the Anderson camp meeting:

> Some of us have been to the International camp meeting quite a number of times; we had placed it next to heaven. But the last year I was there quite a few of our people came from the south and we were so happy, but a few of the Brethren called for us to meet them. We went to the appointed place and this is what they told us: "There are too many of your people coming here. You'll hinder the whites from coming and being saved. Why don't you get a place of your own?" . . . Our hearts were made sad and many tears were shed, for we had no place to go. But later we heard of the meeting here and again our hearts were made to rejoice that we had a place where we could assemble and praise God.[23]

Mother Moore is remembered as one of the saints who worked for many years to "keep a door open" at West Middlesex to allow people to assemble and worship God together regardless of race or color.[24] Yet the West Middlesex camp meeting was not convened as a response to the racism of the Anderson leaders, because Brother Wimbish had received his vision years before he knew the Church of God ever existed, and the camp meeting was fully operational before the black saints began to experience alienation from the predominantly white Anderson gatherings.

This brief history of the origins of a black Holiness organization demonstrates egalitarian cooperative empowerment of black men and women. On their own turf, so to speak, these black men and women rejected the racist social ethics of the white "saints" and assumed the morally consistent position of refusing to exclude others on the basis of race or sex. Instead of evoking further exclusive practices, the experience of racism gave them greater light on the importance of maintaining an open door. Consistent with their understanding of Christian love, they were guided more by an ethics of inclusion than by a desire for racial solidarity.

Cherokee Charismatic Revival preceded this.
— Perry Stone

Charismatic Cooperation:
The Azusa Street Revival

The story of the 1906 Azusa Street Revival, which marks the beginning of Pentecostalism as an international movement, suggests a charismatic model of cooperative ministry and empowerment among the sexes, where authority and recognition are granted to either sex based upon the exercise of spiritual gifts. The early Pentecostal movement was led by William J. Seymour, a man whose own life story reflects practically all major facets of the denominational racism experienced by black Christians in the United States.[25] Born in Louisiana in 1878, Seymour was raised as a Baptist, as a young man joined a local black congregation of the Methodist Episcopal Church in Indianapolis, Indiana, and next was drawn to the Evening Light Saints, a name widely used at the time for the Church of God (Anderson, Indiana).

After joining the Holiness movement, Seymour came under the influence of a black woman pastor in Houston, Texas, Lucy Farrow, attending her church in 1903. Significantly, she was the first to expose Seymour to the practice of speaking in tongues:

> He heard a woman pray aloud in a language, or what seemed to be a language, that no one there could understand. Seymour was touched to the core. As a man of prayer himself, he could sense that this woman had somehow attained a depth of spiritual intensity he had long sought but never found. . . . These experiences changed Seymour's life. After the meeting he asked Lucy Farrow, the woman who had spoken in the strange tongue, more about her remarkable gift.[26]

Farrow introduced Seymour to the white Pentecostal pioneer Charles Fox Parham, who ran a Bible school in Topeka for missionaries where she had worked as a "governess." When Seymour enrolled in Parham's classes in Houston, he was subjected to the indignity of having to sit in a hall where he could hear the classes through the doorway, in keeping with Southern "etiquette." Seymour accepted Parham's advocacy of tongues-speaking, but rejected his racist prejudices and polemics.

Seymour's work with women ministers continued. He was invited by Neely Terry, a Holiness woman from Los Angeles, to pastor a Holiness congregation in California that had been founded by Julia W. Hutchins. Seymour traveled to Los Angeles bearing the message that speaking in tongues was the necessary evidence of the Pentecostal experience, but Hutchins rejected his preaching and locked him out. He found refuge in the home of Richard and Ruth Asberry on Bonnie Brae Street, where he conducted several weeks of prayer meetings. When on April 9, 1906 Seymour finally manifested the tongue-speaking experience he had promoted in his preaching, a revival broke out and crowds began to gather at the Bonnie Brae Street residence and in the streets. He leased a vacant building at 312 Azusa Street in Los Angeles from the Stevens African Methodist Episcopal Church (where several persons worshiping with him had formerly been members), a two-story wooden structure located in a poor black neighborhood in Los Angeles, near some stables and a lumberyard. Within a few days more than a thousand persons were trying to enter the small mission building, and the Azusa Street Revival was under way. The core group consisted primarily of black female domestic workers, but over a period of three years, from 1906 to 1908, the Revival drew persons of every race, nationality, and culture.

On the surface, this account of the Azusa Street Revival presents an all-too-familiar image of a black man leading a congregation of black women that seems less than empowering from the vantage point of gender. To designate this model as "charismatic," however, is to add the perspective that the Revival resulted from the partnership of women and men unified by their desire to experience the spiritual empowerment of speaking in tongues. Seymour was largely mentored, guided, and offered a context for ministry by women. Women were involved in every aspect of his spiritual development; moreover, women were willing to follow his tongues doctrine and experience its full effects as a public witness. In this light, the locus of empowerment was not the cooperation of men and women with each other as an end in itself. Rather, the people were spiritually empowered by their ability to respond to charismatic leadership, a process facilitated by the willingness of one man to welcome the participation and preaching of women. And when the desired spiritual manifestations came forth among this humble gathering, the experience of corporate charismatic empowerment drew attention from all parts of the world.

That a man led this movement is perhaps unremarkable; that he was so heavily influenced by women's spiritual leadership is hardly unprecedented. What is highly unusual here, however, is the immediate interracial and international impact produced by this tiny core group of black women and men. Together they exercised charismatic gifts in a manner that would alter the course of church history throughout the twentieth century. Today Pentecostalism has become the dominant expression of Christian worship in many major urban centers, claiming some 410 million adherents worldwide.[27]

Theologian William C. Turner, Jr. has interpreted Seymour's view of the relationship between charismatic spirituality and race in ethical and theological terms:

> The coming together of the races was the act for which the revival was a sign of approbation. Indeed, the approbation of Azusa Street, in Seymour's view, had more to do with the crossing of racial lines and the achievement of unity in the body of Christ than the formal criterion of glossolalia as proof of spirit baptism. In this respect, Seymour was more within the tradition of the African American religious experience than anything else.[28]

Seymour eventually encountered many negative experiences with white participants in the Revival who did not share his perspective on racial unity. When Parham visited Azusa Street at Seymour's invitation in October 1906, he denounced the Revival as a "darky camp meeting."[29] The two white women who helped Seymour to publish the periodical *Apostolic Faith,* with an international circulation of 50,000 subscribers, effectively destroyed Seymour's publication outreach ministry by taking both the periodical and the mailing list to Portland, Oregon, where one of them founded another evangelistic organization. In his book *Fire from Heaven,* Harvey Cox notes how Seymour's disillusionment with white Pentecostals affected his understanding of the gift of tongues:

> Finding that some people could speak in tongues and continue to abhor their black fellow Christians convinced him that it was not tongue speaking but the dissolution of racial barriers that was the surest sign of the Spirit's pentecostal presence and the approaching New Jerusalem.[30]

Seymour saw the breaking of the color line as a much surer sign than tongue-speaking of God's blessing and of the Spirit's healing presence, signifying that the charismatic ideal of cooperation with the Spirit had become compromised in practice by the forces of racism. Once the whites defected, the Azusa Street Mission became almost entirely black.[31] The denominations that took the lead thereafter to spread the Pentecostal doctrine and practices, for example, the Church of God in Christ and the Assemblies of God, were organized along racial lines and generally assigned subordinate roles to women.

White racism ultimately undermined and destroyed the vision of racial equality promoted by the early Pentecostals. Interracial cooperation could not be sustained within the charismatic leadership structures where cooperation between the sexes had been so conspicuous (at least temporarily). As a result, Seymour revised the doctrines, discipline, and constitution of his Apostolic Faith movement to recognize himself as "bishop" and guarantee that his successor would always be "a man of color."[32] After Seymour's death in 1922, however, it was a woman of color who assumed the leadership of the Mission—his widow, Jennie Seymour. As is often the case after the death of charismatic leaders, the mission located at Azusa Street did not last very long thereafter. The building was demolished in 1931, and the land was lost in foreclosure in 1938, two years after Jennie Seymour's death.[33]

The strategy the black Holiness and Pentecostal pioneers employed in their dealings with whites remains instructive for subsequent generations of black Christians who share his commitment to interracial unity—openness to whites who are accepting of the offer of fellowship, and repudiation of whites whose racism and other moral failings produce alienation and strife within the church. Despite feeling disillusioned by the apostasy of white racists, Seymour apparently reverted to his Holiness roots by remaining resolved to a vision of interracial unity, even as it eluded his grasp and receded into the eschatological future. The egalitarian spirit and fervor remained in evidence in the National Association of the Church of God, even after the men began to dominate leadership roles and women became marginalized as preachers and leaders in later years. In both cases de facto racial separation and female subordination eventually overshadowed the original vision.

The Dialectical Model: Women in the Church of God in Christ

The largest denomination of the Holiness-Pentecostal tradition, the Church of God in Christ (COGIC), does not permit the ordination of women but has the most powerful Women's Department of any black denomination.[34] Despite this restriction, women have exercised ministerial leadership in numerous ways, serving as evangelists, worship leaders, and religious activists, and sometimes having charge of churches in the absence of a male pastor. The distinctive leadership orientation of the COGIC women led to levels of female empowerment and male-female cooperation that would prove vital to the success of the denomination throughout the twentieth century, in contrast to the Azusa Street Mission, which failed after the death of Seymour. Cheryl

Townsend Gilkes has offered this general observation regarding the importance of the establishment of structures of female "influence" as a determining factor in the survival of black religious movements:

> Although many denominations were formed between 1895 and 1950, those that survived and flourished were those with strong Women's Departments. Structures of female influence enabled denominations with charismatic male founders to grow after those founders died; other denominational movements with high visibility but no structures of female influence almost disappeared.[35]

The Women's Department of the COGIC was formed shortly after the beginning of the Azusa Street Revival. Bishop Charles H. Mason, a former Baptist minister who with C. P. Jones founded the COGIC as a Holiness denomination, participated in the Revival and received the gift of speaking in tongues. As a result, a split occurred with Jones and the COGIC became Pentecostal under Mason's leadership in 1907. Around the same time, Mason recruited Lizzie Woods Roberson from a Baptist academy to organize the Women's Department as its "overseer." What is unusual about this development is that Mason was divorced, and thus did not have a wife to appoint to this position, as normally occurred in other black denominations where the women's organizations are led by the wives of ecclesial leaders:

> This historical "accident" generated the model of a nearly autonomous women's organization. Mason not only recruited Mother Roberson to head the women's work but also on her advice appointed women's overseers along the same jurisdictional and district lines as the male overseers who later became bishops. The title "overseer," a literal translation of the Greek word usually translated as "bishop," was used in the early days of the church for both men and women leaders in the church. Such usage implied that the founders of the COGIC and other denominations initially envisioned a church organized in parallel structures of both male and female overseers.[36]

Adoption of the terminology associated with episcopally governed churches reflected both the Baptist roots of their leadership and a Presbyterian tendency toward "more or less sharing power between the laity and the clergy."[37] Gilkes has determined that these black churchwomen transformed their autonomy into a form of power best described as "influence," and "created a pluralist political structure in an episcopally governed church where pluralism was never intended."[38] This autonomous, parallel structure more closely resembled the dual sex political systems characteristic of some West African societies than the patriarchal episcopal polities of European origin. The women employed distinctive leadership styles and methods that promoted broader-based participation:

> The women's methods of leadership have evolved in direct contrast to the authoritarian style demanded by the nature of episcopal polity: hierarchical, individualistic, and dominating. In comparison, women's leadership tends to be consensus oriented, collective, and more inclusive, involving larger numbers of people in decision making.[39]

The emergence of the COGIC Women's Department was timely in view of the plight of black women in church and society during the first decade of the twentieth century. First, the spiritual and professional focus of this organization of black women produced significant affirmations of black female personhood:

> In the face of cultural assaults that used the economic and sexual exploitation of black women as a rationale for their denigration, the Sanctified Church elevated black women to the status of visible heroines—spiritual and professional role models for their churches.[40]

A second factor is the professionalization of Christian education (in contrast to the concurrent marginalization of Christian education by Baptist and Methodist denominations), which enabled women to use their roles as educators and the "educated" as a source of power and career opportunity. Third, the Women's Department presented "professional" role models for black working women, at a time when employment opportunities for black women were primarily restricted to domestic service at low wages; thus, "Higher education and work were identified as legitimate means of upward mobility for black women, and they were encouraged to achieve economic empowerment through white-collar employment."[41] An important consequence of this emphasis upon higher education and professional employment was the financial empowerment of women, whose numerical dominance in the churches in turn created a situation that clearly contradicted the ethic of male domination and control.[42]

As a general rule, the Sanctified churches rejected cultural norms and organizational models that imitated white patriarchy. For both the Holiness and the Pentecostal churches, holiness was the premier ethic and guide for liturgy, preaching, and polity:

> Church members could not advance ideologies of patriarchy that contradicted standards of holiness since "holiness" was the most important achieved status in these churches—and a status not humanly conferred. Biblical debate concerning women was confined to structural norms, not the nature, quality, or character of women per se.[43]

The positive affirmation of women's nature, quality, and character sets these churches apart from other Protestant and Catholic traditions whose exclusion of women from leadership is grounded in the rejection of the full humanity of women. As a result, even where structural prohibitions have been in effect, women nevertheless found ways to exercise their gifts of ministry and leadership to the benefit of the entire church body. For example, women evangelists and revivalists founded churches, so they were included in church histories. In addition, male church leaders often reported in their spiritual biographies that they became converted in response to the ministry of female preachers and revivalists. Thus, it was not gender but spiritual gifts that qualified individuals to be acknowledged and honored in Holiness and Pentecostal circles: "the personal and congregational accounts passed down in written records and oral tradition placed a high value on the contribution of women and men to the most important goal of the church—salvation and holiness."[44]

Following Gilkes's analysis, the model of leadership developed by the COGIC Women's Department is a dialectical one, based on a tradition of protest and cooperation.[45] On the one hand, this dialectics is driven by the women's struggle against structures and patterns of subordination based on sex and, on the other, by their determination to maintain unity with black men in the face of racism and discrimination in the larger society, and in response to internal power struggles among male leaders within the denomination. Because cooperative and egalitarian norms govern this dialectical model, the structural exclusion of women from certain positions in the church is partially offset by the maintenance of various spaces and spheres for women to exercise their spiritual gifts and leadership.

Models of Cooperation

Three models have been profiled here to demonstrate alternative means of male-female cooperation in the early history of the Sanctified church tradition. The charismatic model encouraged emulation of a particular individual, toward the end of personal attainment of spiritual power in some special form. The egalitarian model upheld the principle that every believer had equal right or access to spiritual power, regardless of sex, race, or class. The dialectical model was characterized by a tension between protest and cooperation, because women had equal access to charismatic power but were restricted in the exercise of that power within the church. While each of these models of empowerment by cooperation drew strength from the participation of both sexes, none was able to sustain structures of interracial cooperation. Although the prevailing norms of racial and sexual exclusion eventually were brought to bear upon these denominational structures, the Sanctified churches nevertheless provided important opportunities and role models for women's spiritual and social empowerment. These cases and models of empowerment by cooperation challenge the current generation of male and female spiritual leaders in all churches to review current practices in the full light of Holiness and Pentecostal church history.

Achievement

In her book *Beautiful, Also, Are the Souls of My Black Sisters,* a history of black women in America, Jeanne Noble traces the twentieth-century emergence of the college-educated black woman back to the Reconstruction period. As the white New England "schoolmarms" left the South, thousands of black women were trained to take up the task of instructing the former slaves and their children. Noble cites two reasons why more black women than men earned college degrees at this point in history. First, teaching in America had become a female occupation and nonthreatening to white men. Second, black men saw teaching as "woman's work" and "naturally" wanted the diversification of occupations that they knew to be available to white men.[1]

Paula Giddings offers a similar explanation of why black women have achieved more educational and professional advancement than black men in her account of the impact of black women on race and sex in America, *When and Where I Enter:*

> Prejudice against their race and sex forced Black women to work and simultaneously limited the kinds of work they could perform. The only choice Black women had were the professions—or do-

mestic work. Since education is the key to the more attractive occupations, Black women have a history of striving for education beyond what their gender or their color seemed to prescribe. Black men, on the other hand, have not had the same motivation, historically, because they had a greater range of options—including blue-collar work, which often pays better than the traditional women's professions (teaching, social work, nursing, and so on.)[2]

Giddings cites such factors as allegations of black female overachievement, conflicts with black men, family breakups, and associated feelings of guilt and ambivalence as part of the price black women have been forced to pay for the achievement of transcending the double discrimination of racism and sexism. While historically there have been more college-educated and professional black women than men in the general population, black men nevertheless still earn a higher median income than do black women on their same educational level.[3] This is significant because it demonstrates that black women's greater efforts to educate and advance themselves have not eliminated the income gap between women and men.

In 1986 two reporters for the *Washington Post,* Jacqueline Trescott and Dorothy Gilliam, wrote a series of three articles on "The New Black Woman." The series was based upon in-depth interviews of fifty black women across the country and a *Washington Post*/NBC News poll of 582 black women concerning the social and political attitudes. Their research yielded some important statistical information from the 1980 Census and other sources. With regard to higher education, some 60% of the blacks enrolled in colleges are women, and 70% to 80% of the blacks who graduate from college are women, indicative of a continuing trend toward more college-educated women than men within the black population. A somewhat less dramatic educational difference shows up among younger employed blacks—of employed black women between the ages of 25 and 44, 19.8% had completed four years or more of college, as compared with 26.6% of white women and 16.6% of black men. There are, however, nearly two professional black women for every professional black man. The data show that 10.7% of working black women are in professional specialties such as medicine, science, teaching, and engineering—a smaller percentage than for white women (14.6%) but nearly twice the percentage for black men. Another measure of the progress working black women have made over the years is the enormous change in domestic employment; only 4.7% of all working black women were employed as domestics in 1980, as compared with 60% in 1940.[4] In general, the black woman has outperformed both her forebears and her brothers in terms of educational and professional advancement.

Getting the Learning without Losing the Burning

In an effort to explain the achievement gap that exists between black women and men, Trescott and Gilliam have pointed out an important factor that sets the "new" black woman apart from many of their black male peers, namely, a "renewed interest in traditional institutions and avenues, such as education, women's organizations and the church."[5] In particular, the church is seen as a source of identity, refuge, and development for the "new" black woman. Accordingly, 54% of the black female respondents (as compared with 38% of black male respondents) told *Washington Post*/ABC News pollsters that they attended church at least once a week. Trescott and Gilliam cite a 1985 Gallup poll revealing that 45% of black American adults said they attended a church or synagogue, a percentage only slightly higher than church attendance among American adults in general (42%). In both groups, however, more women than men said they worshiped regularly.[6] This implies that the black woman's higher level of interest and participation in the church has helped her to achieve more than the black man in education and the professions.

Further light is shed on this suggestion by the work of sociologist Cheryl Townsend Gilkes on the roles and traditions of women in the Sanctified Church. Refuting the widely-held assumption that the Holiness and Pentecostal groups that comprise the Sanctified Church are havens of anti-intellectual emotionalism for ignorant and uninformed urban blacks, Gilkes has shown that education has been highly valued among the "Saints":

> The Sanctified Church's emphasis on biblical authority made learning "the Word" an important means for living a sanctified life. Educational goals therefore comprised general literacy, biblical literacy, advanced academic and professional achievement, and biblical expository skills, and these goals apparently ranked second in priority after salvation and holiness. The Saints were encouraged to acquire "the learning" without losing "the burning."[7]

This synthesis of religious fervor and academic and professional achievement is attributable to capable women who, because of their sex, were forbidden to serve the church as ordained ministers, elders, and bishops, but who responded by developing alternative structures for leadership and service that emphasized education. Moreover, religious education in the Sanctified Church, as in many other churches, became an arena of female segregation, but ultimately functioned as a "briar patch" of female empowerment apart from the sacred pulpits of male domination. The pragmatic approach pursued by educated and professional Sanctified women to get the "learning" without losing the "burning" of spiritual fervor produced worthy models for the black churches and community:

> Given the overall, sometimes exaggerated, respect and deference that the black community confers on educators, these women have legitimized the image of the "professional" woman throughout the church. As a result, women in the Sanctified Church have established a more differentiated model of social mobility and occupational aspiration than have the men.[8]

This model of social mobility and occupational aspiration is not necessarily unique to Sanctified Church women; similar models have arisen among Baptist, Methodist, and other church women. Clearly Nannie Helen Burroughs and Mary McLeod Bethune are two noteworthy examples of professional black church women from the Baptist and Methodist "mainstream" whose work as educators served as a platform for exercising church and community leadership.[9] The legitimization of the image of the professional woman throughout the church indicates that, despite its tendency to proscribe women's access to ordained clerical roles within its own ranks, the church has helped black women to assume significant leadership in other spheres of influence by promoting their educational and professional development.

Womanist and Christian Ethics: A Wheel Within a Wheel

Several factors have been offered thus far to help explain the discrepancy in educational and professional achievement that exists between black women and men, including: the availability of employment opportunities for black men that required less education but paid more than the professions open to black women (for instance, teaching, nursing, and social work); black men's rejection of these professions as "woman's work"; the early limitation of black women's employment options to domestic work, or to professions requiring higher education; and black women's greater interest and involvement in the church as a vital sphere of leadership development that has legitimized the image of the professional woman and offered gender-specific models of social mobility and occupational aspiration. In addition to these factors, some specific ethical and religious considerations can further explain why black women tend to have a stronger orientation toward educational and professional achievement than black men. Some propose that because black women have a much higher level of participation in the church, they are more likely than black men to be exposed to and influenced by a combination of womanist and Christian ethics that urges them to embrace educational and professional advancement as a morally positive response to the evils of racism, sexism, and poverty.

The notion of womanist ethics is finding currency within a growing body of black and feminist theological discourse. Katie G. Cannon, Toinette Eugene, Cheryl Townsend Gilkes, Jacquelyn Grant, Renita J. Weems, and Delores Williams were among the first black female scholars to make use of the term *womanist* in their theological and ethical writings during the 1980s.[10] In a preface to her collection of womanist prose entitled *In Search of Our Mothers' Gardens,* Alice Walker defines "womanist" as a black feminist or feminist of color who, among other things, is willful, serious, loving, and "committed to survival and wholeness of entire people, male *and* female.[11] This concept from black women's literature and culture has special appeal to theologians and ethicists because its inherent claims seem to ring true in the life experiences of black women in general, and women of faith in particular.

For example, three ethical principles that emerge from Walker's definition would include autonomy, commitment, and love. These principles are evident in the experience of the "new black woman" portrayed in the articles by Trescott and Gilliam. Three characteristics that connect these black female achievers to each other (and distinguish them from their white female and black male counterparts) also correlate closely to the womanist ethical principles of autonomy, commitment, and love:

> What connects the women . . . is their eagerness to be seen as independent women, their dream of trying to modify the ethics of the American marketplace to include sensitivity to women and minorities, and their willingness to sacrifice much of their private lives in pursuit of those goals.[12]

The eagerness of professional black women to be seen as independent is a characteristic expression of womanist autonomy. The dream of trying to modify the ethics of the American marketplace to include sensitivity to women and minorities is indicative of a commitment to survival and wholeness of others. It is a vision of equal opportunity for all persons to freely pursue an improved quality of life. The women's willingness to sacrifice much of their private lives in pursuit of those goals points to a love ethic of unselfish active concern. Love binds autonomy and commitment in a relationship of creative tension, because love motivates the autonomous individual to choose solidarity with others for the sake of group survival and wholeness.

Womanist ethics and Christian ethics are not identical. The attitudes and outlook of these black female achievers, however, bear some distinctively Christian aspects. Most of the black women polled and interviewed in the *Washington Post* series said they attended church. Their Christian ethics is readily and convincingly revealed in their willingness to make personal sacrifices for the sake of others, in their hope for a better life of expanded opportunity for themselves and their children in the future, and, even more importantly, in their tendency not to allow success to rob them of compassion for those who have not "made it," particularly for other blacks who remain trapped in poverty and in crime-ridden inner cities. As persons who have had to struggle against deeply entrenched forces of racism and sexism in pursuit of their educational and professional goals, for the most part they have not embraced these biases and prejudices themselves, or used their positions of authority and power to oppress other individuals and groups. In other words, their orientation generally has not been to "render evil for evil," but rather to "overcome evil with good."

In the fall of 1989 the *Journal of Feminist Studies in Religion* published a roundtable discussion of "Christian Ethics and Theology in Womanist Perspective" featuring my essay with responses by Katie G. Cannon, Emilie M. Townes, M. Shawn Copeland, bell hooks, and Cheryl Townsend Gilkes.[13] Gilkes contributed an insightful assessment of the ethical meaning of Alice Walker's work and the church experiences of black women:

In my reading of Walker, and this would make an excellent ethical study encompassing all of her work, this love is the greatest issue in human existence and the critical point of convergence between her creative thinking and the task of Christian ethics. Like many of us who were raised cuddling against our many mothers and aunts under the African-American preaching tradition, the greatest issue gleaned from those sermons was love. For Walker and many others, still "the greatest of these is love" and all else is commentary.[14]

On the basis of this reflection it is possible to reconstruct the ethical focus of the womanist idea in terms of three principles: autonomy, altruism, and adoration. *Autonomy* is the womanist's bold predisposition to self-assertion. *Altruism* refers to the commitment to the liberation and well-being of others as one's life's priority. *Adoration* describes the worshipful spirit of the womanist as expressed in love for "music, dance, the moon, the Spirit, love, food, roundness, struggle, the folk, and herself," which in turn undergirds active concern for others.[15]

To further visualize the dynamic interrelatedness of these three aspects of the womanist idea in Christian ethical perspective, one can evoke a dynamic model of love ethics in the form of a wheel, with love as its hub, and autonomy, altruism, and adoration as its three spokes. The other essential component of the wheel is the rim, which represents the solidarity of mothers and daughters learning from each other how to respond constructively and creatively to the realities of racist and sexist oppression. In order for this wheel to turn, there must be a dynamic balance among the three spokes, that is, there must be self-love, love of others, and love of the Spirit in appropriate proportions. The spokes radiate power from the center to the periphery. The center or hub of the wheel is the point of empowerment where divine and human love connect. The rim is the locus of inclusive praxis, "where the rubber meets the road." This rim must be broad and strong enough to be inclusive of the entire community.

Using this image, it is possible to envision Christian ethics and womanist ethics as "a wheel within a wheel," in allusion to Ezekiel's prophetic vision (Ezek. 1:16b). This same image has importance in the traditional folk music and preaching of African American Christians, as in the lyrics of the Negro spiritual, "Ezekiel saw de wheel, way up in de middle of de air." Ezekiel's vision can be transposed to signify the relationship between Christian and womanist notions of love. The wheel illustrates the love ethic that forms the ground of Christianity, obligating the believer to love God, neighbor, and self. Christian ethics can be conceptualized as a wheel with love at the hub, and with three spokes radiating from it in three directions simultaneously with proportionate intensity the love of God, love of neighbor, and love of self. The rim of the wheel is the community of faith whose testimony and acts of social concern are directly expressive of these various embodiments of love. This wheel is not static; it is dynamic. It spins and moves and works.

The Pauline formulation of Christian ethics as faith, hope, and love can also be depicted using this dynamic model of love ethics. *Faith* is the willingness to move in response to God, the needs of others, and the demands of the self. *Hope* is the vision that gives assurance and direction to this movement. *Love* is the empowerment to move and be moved on behalf of others. This scheme represents one way of envisioning the relationship between womanist and Christian ethics as a harmonious one, as two wheels sharing the one hub of love, but whose spokes and rims also bear significant similarities, inasmuch as the womanist notions of autonomy, altruism, and adoration correspond to Christian notions of love of self, neighbor, and God. These interfacing wheels represent a dynamic progression toward the empowerment of others, that is, toward wholeness, inclusiveness, the bearing of spiritual fruits, and the exercise of spiritual gifts.

The dual wheel image can also be used to develop awareness of possible areas of discord between Christian and womanist ethics, the points of "friction" that affect the motion of the "wheel within a wheel." For example, sharp differences become apparent when womanist values are juxtaposed with the list of virtues the New Testament presents as the fruit of the Spirit: love, joy, peace, patience, kindness, generosity, faithfulness, gentleness, and self-control (Gal. 5:22–23). On the one hand, it is immediately evident that love, joy, kindness, generosity, and faithfulness are consistent with the womanist idea. But on the other hand, it is a difficult challenge to draw a connection between peace, patience, gentleness, and self-control and the intense audaciousness commended by the womanist concept. To take issue with Katie Cannon's discussion of womanist values in terms of "invisible dignity, quiet grace, and unshouted courage," the mood and energy of the womanist idea is visible, loud, and shouted.[16] It conveys rebelliousness, independence, and the free exercise of prerogatives that defy convention. The womanist idea conveys an insubordinate posture and aggressive energy. It may be that the wheel within the wheel is moving in an opposite direction, creating conditions of friction where one slows down the motion of the other. Or, alternatively, the wheel in the middle may give additional impetus to the other because it moves faster and with more intensity. These seemingly contradictory ethical ideals, however, are embodied in the life and work of several generations of black Christian women who had to confront the barriers of race and sex with a bold womanist posture in order to pursue educational and economic empowerment for themselves and others. It can be argued that the statistical edge black women have gained in some areas of education and professional achievement is actually an institutional manifestation of individual expressions of autonomy, altruism, and adoration of the divine.

Values, Vocation, and Vision: Keys to Success

What are some practical implications of this ethical understanding of black women's successes in higher education and professional employment? Many innovations in public policy would have to take place in order to turn the tide of black male under-achievement as indicated by increasing truancy and attrition in secondary schools, lower rates of college matriculation and graduation, and higher unemployment, incarceration, and homelessness. Yet one of the biggest hindrances to black achievement is a moral-ethical dilemma that increases in financial aid for higher education and in employment opportunities alone cannot remedy. Many inner-city youth, and especially adolescent boys, carry a distinctly anti-academic attitude—they harass those who excel in academics as "nerds" or "brainiacs," while praising and accepting into their peer groups those whose performance in school is mainly a matter of "getting over," that is, using one's wits to get by with the least possible exertion.[17] Instead of preparing themselves academically for legitimate careers, some black youth only aspire to gain "respect" by using and selling drugs, engaging in sexual activity, wearing expensive designer clothes, carrying lethal weapons, and so forth. Perhaps more inner-city churches could reach out to these youth (typically they do not attend church) with religious education ministries designed to arm them with ethics that promote achievement instead of self-destruction. A synthesis of womanist and Christian ethics would include three concepts that could be used to help motivate young blacks, both male and female, to cultivate their intellectual gifts in keeping with the best traditions of black achievement: (1) an emphasis on values, (2) a sense of vocation, and (3) a vision of human progress.

Eleanor Holmes Norton, who has served as Democratic Delegate to Congress representing the District of Columbia, professor at the Georgetown University Law Center, and chairperson of the Equal Employment Opportunity Commission, is herself a paragon of black female achievement and advocacy. She has written about the need to reinforce black families by passing on the "enduring values that form the central content of the black American heritage": hard work, education, respect for family, and achieving a better life for one's children.[18] It is by hard work, and not by "getting over," that honorable people earn a living for themselves and their families.

Education, according to Gilkes, has represented a "supreme cultural value in the black church and community."[19] It remains the principal vehicle available to blacks for acquiring gainful employment and overcoming the poverty and degradation of ghetto life. Moreover, education prepares blacks to compete, racist and sexist discrimination notwithstanding, for the best employment opportunities available.

Respect for family implies giving highest priority to family ties and obligations, especially those that bond parents to children. This value especially needs to be emphasized within those communities where fathers are typically absent from the family circle. Respect for family is of critical importance insofar as the family functions as a vital support network for the individual who aspires to achieve. In fact, it can be argued that participation in the family is as significant a factor as participation in the church in accounting for the differences between black men and women in educational and professional attainments.

Sociologist Joyce Ladner, who has dedicated much of her professional career to seeking solutions to the problems facing poor blacks, has stated that she has "not met a poor black mother over the past 20 years who did not want her children to do better in life than she did."[20] Ladner seems correct in her perception that the desirability of achieving a better life for one's children persists as an important value in the black community; however, at the same time she laments the fact that parental aspirations do not always translate into real opportunity for black youth. She illustrates the inability of black youth to pursue higher education and indicts the larger society for supplying the materialistic values and allurements leading to their downfall:

> Unfortunately, children aren't influenced that much by their parents' dreams unless the parents can help them to achieve them. Poor children soon realize their parents cannot afford to send

them to college if they can't always pay the rent or keep the food from running out before payday. A 17-year-old told me he stopped dreaming of going to college when he turned 16. "By then I knew it was all over," he said.

Dashed dreams lead quickly to cynicism, hopelessness and despair. Unable to climb the ladder of legitimate success, young people are more easily lured into the fast lane of selling drugs for quick cash. Expensive [items] . . . help to boost the flagging self-esteem of young people who feel they cannot achieve otherwise and who find reinforcement for that belief in the materialistic values of the larger society.[21]

Even more disturbing is Ladner's observation that the moral and ethical disorientation of inner-city communities is such that violence, bloodshed, and a wanton disregard for human life is commonplace among adolescents. This new culture in which life is "up for grabs" threatens to subvert what is perhaps the single most critical sustaining value of the black community: the sanctity of human life. Ladner proposes several solutions to this moral-ethical dilemma, including some that would call upon the churches to help young people by promoting education and other values in a manner suggestive of womanist Christian ethics. For example, she suggests that churches and other institutions open their doors for after-school "learning centers" where youths can have a structured place to do their homework, and that they do more to teach young people how to handle conflict and stress without resorting to violence, that is, to teach them the practical application of the Christian ethic of nonviolence.

In 1982 George Davis and Glegg Watson published a study of black participation in American corporations entitled *Black Life in Corporate America: Swimming in the Mainstream.* A chapter of that book focused upon the experience and insights of black women in the corporate sector. One of the distinctive characteristics of this select group of black female achievers was their tendency to temper personal ambition with a desire to "wrestle with social and human problems in the way that most corporate men and some women . . . did not want to do."[22] Trescott and Gilliam discovered a similar sense of vocation among the black professional women they interviewed. Many of these women, however, expressed feelings of guilt due to their failure to maintain close enough proximity to low-income areas to fulfill this perceived calling to serve as role models for the so-called black underclass. This sense of personal and collective guilt over the unrealized social role of the black middle class in relation to the black underclass is seen as "one of the hallmarks of the new black woman—one with fewer apparent parallels among their white or male colleagues."[23] The promotion of values to enhance achievement among black youth clearly ought to include an orientation to keep in mind the plight of the less privileged in the course of one's pursuit of the opportunities and options afforded by academic success. In this regard, the black female achievers' sense of vocation is strongly reminiscent of both the womanist commitment to survival and wholeness of entire people, and the Christian commitment to follow the example of Jesus in showing concern for the poor. The inclination of educated black women to become involved in "uplifting" the black community is rooted in the educational experience of the freed slaves in the nineteenth century.

Womanist ethicist Toinette Eugene has noted that the black freedwoman "was taught that her education was meant not only to uplift her but also to prepare her for a life of service in the overall community."[24] Reflecting upon the inspiration black women received earlier in the twentieth century from Bethune and Burroughs, Eugene lifts up a diaconal model of servant leadership (as espoused by Christ) focused on solidarity with those who suffer or who are marginalized in any way.[25]

It is virtually impossible to achieve a goal without having a mental picture of it, that is, without a vision of that goal. One of the critical shortcomings of the current generation of troubled black youth is their lack of vision with regard to either personal achievement or the collective progress of black people. Davis and Watson have made a very interesting observation concerning the distinctive manner in which corporate black women envision their own progress, stating that "they undoubtedly knew intimately what their mothers and grandmothers had had to go through, and so their mood and energy seemed to reflect how far they, collectively, had come, rather than how far they had to go."[26] This implies that the vision that motivates these black women has as its focus a sense of carrying forward both the struggles and triumphs of their foremothers. This vision connects past tradition with future hope, and also generates the appropriate "mood and energy" to undertake the tasks of the present.

In similar terms, ethicist Preston Williams has set forth a black ethic of achievement that is rooted first in the mastery of self-understanding, that is, in coming to know what it means to be black in a white-dominated but multiracial world, and is "carried by the hope that all men [and women] can and will become achievers, i.e., sharers in the task of providing abundant life for all persons."[27] In order to excel in academics and in the professions, black women have not only had to master an understanding of themselves as blacks in a white-dominated world, but also have needed to divest themselves of any illusion that there is no disadvantage in being female in a male-dominated world. The prospect of participating in the process of bringing about equal access to abundant life is perhaps the best hope and the highest calling that womanist Christian ethics has to offer the present generation of black youth—it is clearly the greatest challenge.

Remoralization
6

The approaches to empowerment ethics discussed thus far have primarily been drawn from the activity of black Christian women who have reached out to meet the spiritual and material needs of the poor. While men certainly have been represented among those giving and receiving help in this regard, especially in the specialized outreach of the urban churches and rescue missions, participants in the service organizations and missionary societies who have sought the empowerment of the poor have been largely female. Although men have dominated the leadership roles in the black churches, the vast majority of their followers have been women.

The challenge of confronting and overcoming barriers of class has taken a different course within the community of black men. Few African American males have bridged the gap between the poor and middle classes in the same manner as Anna Julia Cooper or Mary McLeod Bethune. The male civil rights leaders are better known for their outspoken advocacy on behalf of the poor than for actually feeding or educating them. In most churches, "missionary" work is women's work. Still, the official public discourse concerning religion and ethics in the African American community has been conducted mostly by males.

Indisputably, the dominant figure in the modern history of African American social ethical leadership is Martin Luther King, Jr. He forcefully affirmed the dignity of black and poor and oppressed people as a civil rights leader and as a Christian prophet. But is there anything in his ethics that speaks to the moral accountability of oppressed people to each other, and to the individuals, communities, and structures that constitute the society at large?

A Tale of Two Kings:
Martin's Dream and Rodney's Nightmare

One approach to this question is to compare Martin King's version of the American dream as a vision of peace, freedom, and equality, with the American nightmare of Rodney King, the African American male motorist who was brutally beaten by a group of Los Angeles police officers in 1991. An amateur videotape of this beating was widely aired by the major television networks for days and weeks after the event occurred, a factor that spurred public outrage in response to the acquittal of the accused police officers by an all-white suburban jury. As a result, much of South Central Los Angeles erupted into flames, and more than fifty lives were lost. To construct a tale of two Kings is to envision two men victimized by a racist society, whose victimization sparked urban conflagration and outrage in the most depressed areas of America's inner cities. Both Kings expressed the desire for racial reconciliation—Martin in an eloquent sermon on the steps of the Lincoln Memorial preached in the summer of 1963 at the historic March on Washington, and Rodney in the form of a question feebly uttered at a nationally televised press conference as South Central Los Angeles went up in smoke: "Can't we all just get along?"

Many middle-class African Americans have realized Martin Luther King's dream through economic empowerment. Their children go to the best public and private schools alongside white, Asian, and Hispanic children, increasing numbers of them live in integrated suburban housing, and their employment is more likely to be in the mainstream public and private sector than in black businesses or institutions. Yet Rodney King's experience is a reminder that justice still eludes those whom the society fears on the basis of their color, culture, and sex. His nightmare has two parts, of course—first, the initial arrest and beating, then the acquittal of those responsible by an all-white suburban jury. The videotape repeatedly shown on television indicates that the Los Angeles police officers committed a gross violation of King's basic human rights. But who has addressed the question of Rodney King's own sphere of moral accountability, as a man whose behavior included the habitual use of drugs and alcohol and disregard of the rights and property of others? Does the Christian church have anything to offer to the Rodney Kings of this world other than to defend their right not to be subjected to police brutality? Does any aspect of Martin King's legacy speak to black male accountability to their own neighbors and women and parents and children?

Readings of King's Legacy

A review of ethical and biographical studies of Martin Luther King reveals some distinct differences between black and white assessments of his ethical leadership and legacy. Black male writers have tended to emphasize King's public triumphs and moral vision. White male writers agonize over King's private sins, and his struggles as bearer of the cross of America's conscience.[1] While some of the black male writers do concede that King was no saint in this regard, they seem to stumble over the question of his relation to women and attitudes toward female leadership. Dealing with the problem of King's incarnation of his ideals requires more than a footnote or disclaimer, as is given in most of these works. No useful purpose seems to be served by dwelling upon the details of King's transgressions, which is why Ralph Abernathy's book *And the Walls Came Tumbling Down* created such an uproar when it was published in 1986. Lewis Baldwin does devote a few pages to assessing the damage done by David Garrow, Taylor Branch, Abernathy, and others who have raised questions concerning King's moral and intellectual integrity. He attempts to lay the matter to rest with the conclusion that

> Whatever the case, no assessment of King's weaknesses as a symbol should occur without a recognition of his vast repertoire of virtues, the most important among which was his willingness to put human concerns and basic human values above personal fame and wealth.[2]

Ethicists and theologians who ignore or mask King's moral errors in the effort to honor his legacy can be blinded by their own biases in this regard. For example, on the matter of plagiarism, King's occasional appropriation of the ideas and words of others without attribution necessarily skews the outcome of studies that seek to bring him into dialogue with the great white ethicists, theologians, and social theorists. By the same token, some are inclined to err by overlooking King's own dealings with women while attempting to portray him as an advocate for the rights and status of women.

It is difficult to discern what should be condoned and what should be condemned in sorting out the facts of King's life. After all is said and done, if indeed that day ever comes, King did succeed in the incarnation of some of his greatest ideas, and he certainly ought to be remembered as a man who was willing to sacrifice his life in the pursuit of lofty ideals toward the end of promoting the well-being of others. He sought, however imperfectly, freedom, justice, and community, not only for his own people, but for oppressed people everywhere. The fact that he discerned and responded to human need by calling national and global attention to Christian ethical discourse through mass mobilization for nonviolent resistance to produce social change challenges modern-day African American Christian intellectuals to "go and do likewise."

Womanist Responses to King's Ethics and Ideals

What critique does the womanist perspective bring to bear upon African American male ethical leadership in light of Martin King's legacy and Rodney King's fate? The womanist concept begins with the notion of black feminism.[3] If feminism means advocacy of the equal rights and status of women, then womanism is advocacy for the equal rights and status of black women. Thus the critical point of womanist inquiry would be to ask whether African American male ethical leaders exhibit respect for the rights, status, and roles of women as partners in the struggle against oppression and injustice. The testimony of some is that Martin King did not readily accept women as equals within the leadership ranks of the civil rights movement.[4]

To be sure, many African American women seeking acceptance and support as church and community leaders have been hindered and hurt by African American male ethical leaders who doubt the equality and ability of their female counterparts. The womanist concept connotes black women taking an assertive posture of leading rather than passively following *en masse*. Aside from the question of whether women should be assertive or not, the issue relevant to both men and women in light of the King leadership paradigm is whether the eloquent, charismatic, authoritative preacher is the best leadership style or model for the empowerment of the masses of people. In this regard, Fannie Lou Hamer, Ella Baker, and Jo Ann Robinson are of great importance as models of assertive female leadership on the grassroots level, but King did not seem to give them much credit or respect as leaders. In keeping with the womanist idea, these women were "responsible, in charge, serious" leaders, but during the civil rights movement much was said and done to put men in the forefront and women in the back. This is ironic in view of Rosa

Parks's adamant refusal to take a back seat on the bus, an action without which there may have been no Montgomery bus boycott and no subsequent mobilization of people to demand racial equality throughout the South. The womanist idea includes a statement of commitment to survival and wholeness of entire people, male and female. Moreover, the womanist is not a separatist. Thus, womanist thought would prod African American male ethical leaders toward the formation of a more inclusive community where relations between the sexes are not characterized by domination, discrimination, or denial of each other's humanity. In the chapter "Martin Luther King and Womanist Theology" in his book *King among the Theologians,* Noel Erskine offers a highly speculative discussion of the dialogue that would have taken place between King and the womanist theologians and ethicists. He fails to direct critical attention, however, to what actually occurred as King interacted with women in the civil rights movement.[5]

In any case, the multifaceted, unconditional love ethic of the womanist, including love of the folk and love of herself, resonates readily with the manner in which King sought to connect love inextricably with justice. As Preston Williams has observed,

> While white and black Christians for years before King stated that love was an effective agent for social change, they applied it only to interpersonal relations and not to issues of social justice. . . . King, unlike many another love ethicist, sought to make love an essential aspect of both the private and public sectors, individual and group life. In theory and practice he made love count in the operationalization of the concept of justice.[6]

Womanist ethicist Katie G. Cannon strives to connect the moral perspective and plight of the celebrated black women writer Zora Neale Hurston with the black church ethics articulated by King and Howard Thurman:

> Taking seriously the theological tradition of the Black Church means that Black women can enhance their experiential moral wis-

dom. Neither Howard Thurman nor Martin Luther King, Jr. reflect directly on the Black woman's experience, but emergent in their theologies is the strong affirmation of the dignity of all Black people grounded in God.[7]

She insists upon the continuing relevance of King's ethics to black women's future struggles: "Black women today must embrace the formal features of the theological ethics of Thurman and King because they provide moral resources for the great struggle that *still lies ahead*."[8]

In her article "Ethics for Living a Dream Deferred," womanist ethicist Marcia Riggs begins to construct a black liberation ethic that explicitly addresses the concerns of women, using as a primary source the contributions of four nineteenth-century African American female leaders: Julia Foote, Maria Stewart, Anna Julia Cooper, and Ida B. Wells-Barnett. She finds in the words of Foote, Stewart, Cooper, and Wells-Barnett several features of black women's race-class-gender consciousness:

> An awareness of a connection between the oppression of Blacks and women in terms of power and justice; an acknowledgment of the distinctive aspects of oppression for black women and men; the recognition of an interrelationship between the oppression of Blacks in America and other people of color; an evaluation of the relation between economics and justice in American society; and a belief in both the justice of God and justice for Blacks as a command of God.[9]

In the process of bringing a critical womanist perspective to bear upon some of the same ethical ideas finding expression in the thought of Martin King, Riggs lifts up intragroup social responsibility as a core value for black liberation ethics, and inclusiveness as a core value for a new ethical paradigm of social responsibility for the American society as a whole:

> In the black community, we must formulate and execute an ethic for black liberation which offers a means for mediating between accommodative and aggressive political activism, between reli-

gious radicalism for and the socio-economics of societal change, between progress for individual Blacks and progress for Blacks as a group.

Intragroup social responsibility represents a core value for the formulation of this ethic, and the socio-ethical tradition of black women must be gleaned for the retrieval of insights as to the content of this core value. In American society overall, the resolution of our ethical dilemmas requires that we conceive a new ethical paradigm of social responsibility—one that has inclusiveness as its core value.[10]

The two "core values" she identifies within the desired ethic of the black community and American society can be seen as one and the same, depending upon the vision one holds for the future self-understanding of the two respective groups. Inclusiveness can mean the same thing as intragroup social responsibility if blacks are seen as Americans; to include them in the larger group ushers all into the realm of intragroup social responsibility, based upon the assumption that an authentically liberative paradigm pushes blacks and other Americans toward the common ground of community.

Intragroup Social Responsibility and Black Moral Leadership

This discussion of intragroup social responsibility leads precisely to the point where attention should be shifted back to the nightmare of Rodney King. This King not only lived a nightmare of police brutality, but the aftermath of the trial produced a nightmare of urban rebellion for all of America. An examination of King's previous and subsequent encounters with police reveals, however, that he embodies in his own behavior the worst nightmares of others in the society, and not just the police. Rodney King was victimized, and the acquittal of his assailants evoked an incredible outpouring of rage and destruction. But if it can be agreed that police brutality is an inappropriate way of dealing with Rodney King, the question remains: What role, if any, does a man like him play in the search for community? What contribution can he make to discussions of intragroup social responsibility and inclusiveness, considered locally, nationally, or globally? Is it anyone's responsibility to reach out to Rodney King and invite him into ethical dialogue, or even to alter his antisocial behavior? Who can lead Rodney King? What, if any, impact can African American male ethical leadership have upon the moral empowerment of Rodney King and others like him?

The issue of black moral leadership has been addressed in debates between liberal and conservative black intellectuals. Among the black conservatives who came to prominence during the Reagan years is Glenn C. Loury, who has argued that the traditional civil rights leadership has failed to provide moral leadership for poor inner-city blacks, who needed to change their behavior in order to escape the crime and poverty of the ghetto. Liberal thinkers such as Cornel West have criticized the black conservatives for placing too much emphasis upon the moral irresponsibility of some blacks, and too little upon the moral responsibility of the society at large in accounting for the persistence of poverty and crime in the inner cities. Still, too few African American male ethicists and theologians are willing to engage in normative discourse on the intragroup level with reference to these same problems.

One reason for this is that some black intellectuals cannot bring themselves to address the problem of moral leadership with specific reference to such crises as disintegration of the family, high homicide rates, and use of alcohol and drugs, because they find it difficult or impossible to draw upon Martin King's life and legacy to substantiate prescriptive analysis in this arena. But Rodney King symbolizes a genuine threat to community on several levels, including behavior he has initiated himself, the violent manner in which police and others have responded to him, and the mass destruction of life and property evoked by his victimization. Ethicists who analyze the one King must also give consideration to the other. Rodney King's case presses the issue of altering the public discourse to address intragroup concerns in the interest of our collective survival as a people and as a nation.

Notwithstanding whatever critique might be brought to bear upon ethicists and ethical leaders, white or black, male or female, with respect to questions of intragroup social responsibility, Rodney King must be given credit for taking the initiative to engage in the quest for community. When he stood before the press in the spring of 1992 and asked the people of Los Angeles, "Can't we all just get along?" his inquiry probed the social-ethical consciousness of America and the world. This King had no gifts of eloquence or articulation, but the simple question he set before the nation forms an appropriate point of departure for African American male ethical leaders to refashion Martin King's quest for community in terms that can answer the particular threats and challenges encountered now as America moves toward the twenty-first century.

From Demoralization to Remoralization

"Remoralization" is offered here as a new name for the process by which African American men and women can provide empowering responses to Rodney King's question in keeping with the moral vision of Martin King. It is derived from the term *demoralization,* which was coined by the great nineteenth-century lexicographer Noah Webster. In Webster's dictionary, *demoralize* has three meanings:

> 1. to corrupt the morals of: *The drug habit demoralizes its victims.*
> 2. To weaken the spirit, courage, discipline or staying power of; as hunger and cold *demoralized* the army. 3. to confuse or disorder mentally; as, the examiner's questions *demoralized* the applicant.[11]

To remoralize, then, means:

> 1. to restore to a morally sound condition: *The prayer habit remoralizes those who embrace it.* 2. to strengthen the spirit, courage,

discipline and staying power of: *Love and acceptance remoralized the men in the single fathers' support group.* 3. to enable creative problem-solving through restoration of mental clarity and order: *The adult mentor's close supervision remoralized the adolescent.*

An essential motif undergirding this definition of remoralization is the interrelatedness of personal and social transformation. It seems that the concept of transformation has at least two dimensions or arenas of application—the personal and the social. In the religious context, one can be personally transformed and socially disengaged, or personally unchanged and socially conscious. This is one way of drawing distinctions between liberals and conservatives among Christians—the liberals lift up salvation through social justice and the conservatives lift up salvation through family values.

The work of biblical scholar John Gammie further informs this proposal. In his book *Holiness in Israel,* he summarizes his own study of holiness in the Old Testament in relation to three groups of leaders in ancient Israel:

> Diversity within unity is to be discerned in the fact that for the different groups of religious persons within Israel—prophets, priests, and sages—the kind of cleanness required by holiness varied. For the prophets it was a cleanness of social justice, for the priests a cleanness of proper ritual and maintenance of separation, for the sages it was a cleanness of inner integrity and individual moral acts.[12]

Gammie's three-dimensional understanding of biblical holiness in terms of social justice, personal piety, and wisdom or intellectual purity harmonizes with the three parts of the definition of remoralization. To restore to a morally sound condition is the task of the priestly pursuit of cleanness; to strengthen one's spirit, courage, discipline, and staying power is the fruit of the sapiential quest for inner integrity; and to enable creative problem-solving through restoration of mental clarity and order is both a prerequisite for and product of social justice.

Gammie holds that "no claim of exclusive apprehension of holiness and the requirements of holiness is possible for any one of the three groups."[13] This implies that it is possible to strive for integrity in terms of all three ways of becoming holy. The more common tendency, though, is to embrace one to the exclusion (and sometimes derision) of any of the others. For example, "I am for social justice, so the personal and academic concerns are irrelevant." Or, "I am into personal salvation and morality, so I am unperturbed by the social conditions or academic productions." Or, "I am an intellectual, so that as long as I do my research with integrity and write my papers with proper footnotes, I have no need to be engaged in the pursuit of piety or social action."

Remoralization and Reconciliation

These reflections posit a special challenge for persons who would promote empowerment ethics for the African American community. Is the ethic of social, personal, and intellectual remoralization an impossible ethic? If so, which one mode of empowerment, if any, should be pursued most fervently?

Wilson J. Moses, whose specialty is American studies, has addressed ethical questions in several of his analyses of African American leaders. In an article entitled "Civil Religion and the Crisis of Civil Rights," Moses deals with the ways in which African Americans have appealed historically to civil religion in the struggle for civil rights. He concludes that blacks would have to isolate themselves from the negative morality of American liberalism in order to fulfill the moral role prescribed and pursued by Martin King:

> If it were possible for black Americans to isolate themselves from the hedonism, self-indulgence and subjectivism that are fast becoming the American liberal creed, it might be possible for them to serve as the saving remnant of American values. Martin Luther

King, in his *Stride toward Freedom,* expressed the hope that the struggles of black Americans would become the conscience of America and the world. But I do not believe that it is fair to ask black Americans to be the guardians of America's cultural and moral health. Healthy living can be burdensome, as can all forms of righteousness. In any case, black Americans are not more righteous than any other ethnic or racial group, difficult though it may be to reject the myth of black moral exceptionalism. It does not seem likely that black people are willing to sacrifice the American dream in order to fulfill the prophetic role that Martin Luther King wished on them.[14]

Moses claims that the only hope for reform in America is to regain the "tough-minded puritanism, sobriety, and ascetic spirit of the abolition movement and the social gospel, which have served so well in the past as the basis of civil religion, civil rights, and progressive movements in church and in state."[15] In view of this claim, it is difficult to imagine how a remoralization process could be initiated and sustained outside the church. Churches that promote personal and moral transformation as fundamental to the experience of salvation can be the most effective in modeling and replicating the moral reforms Moses is calling for. But Moses follows the lead of Alexander Crummell, Francis Grimke, and other prominent African American male religious leaders in the rejection of those forms and expressions of black folk religion that can be characterized as escapist, overly emotional, and otherworldly. It is clear, however, that there must be a strong and explicit contextualization of spiritual formation and empowerment in order for the remoralization process to succeed.

It is imperative to attempt to relate this notion of remoralization to the concerns of the middle-class Christians who comprise most of the leadership and membership of the black churches. The remoralization concept is presented here as an approach to formulating a collective response to the alienated and self-destructive state of the disinherited African American male, that is, of those demoralized by poverty, its environment, and its effects. But the remoralization of the economically and education-ally empowered African American male is also critical to the continued growth and development of the black church as a re-sourceful institution. How does one prepare a people morally for the acquisition of wealth and exercise of power? What is the logi-cal conclusion of the quest for jobs and economic opportunity in America, if not an affluent lifestyle and the attendant values and beliefs? If the tendency of those with wealth is to distance them-selves from poor neighborhoods, churches, and people, how does one teach, preach, and promote reconciliation between the affluent and the poor within the African American community?

The church is the vital locus for the remoralization and recon-ciliation of male and female, rich, poor, and middle-class persons of all ages, races, and cultural backgrounds seeking to build com-munity. Sociologist Harold Dean Trulear has proposed that in order for the black middle-class church to be reconciled to the underclass, it must build community by seeking ongoing partner-ships in ministry in a spirit of mutuality and not paternalism. In other words, the church must not just go to help the poor, but must also enter into loving relations with "them," who are really "us."[16] Trulear holds the view that the black church plays a unique role as a partner in national and global ethical dialogue, on the basis of its "combination of acquired spiritual, financial, educational and technological resources, along with a keen mem-ory (and sometimes contemporary experience) of what it feels like to be oppressed."[17] His characterization of the ethical di-lemma of the black middle class echoes the stated concern for interpreting the civil rights legacy in light of womanist models of leadership, and for engaging a transformative paradigm in the formulation of an agenda for empowerment and social change:

> The issue, simply put, is this: Was the goal of the Civil Rights Movement placing Black faces in high places, or was it the inten-tion of men like Martin Luther King, Jr. and women like Fannie Lou Hamer that African Americans would bring to an integrated

society the positive social and cultural values which have been forged in the crucible of slavery and segregation and which had a lot to teach white America? If integration is merely the opportunity for Blacks to get good jobs and live where they want to live, then what has really been gained? If a company's business practices are unjust, does it really matter that it has significant Black presence in senior and middle management? If a university offers a curriculum that writes off the Black experience, does it really matter that it has significant Black presence among faculty and administration (or for that matter, on the basketball team)? If the mayor is Black and city services are still poor, where is the benefit of integration? It is transformation and not participation that is at the root of the African American spirituality.[18]

Whether or not one is fully persuaded by the remoralization paradigm, the church must offer some sort of transformative paradigm if it is to take the lead in building a community where men who behave like Rodney King can be reconciled with men who think like Martin King.

The Remoralized Black Male:
Cases in Point

A further illustration of the remoralization concept emerges from the autobiography of El-Hajj Malik El-Shabazz (Malcolm X), an African American male who was neither middle-class nor Christian but who provides a compelling image of manhood for African American youth.[19] One striking contrast between Shabazz and Martin King, a comparison inspired in part by James Cone's book *Martin and Malcolm and America* and Spike Lee's 1992 film *Malcolm X*, is the personal transformation motif. Soon after the film was released, there were many young people on the streets wearing the film's "X" logo on hats and T-shirts, but there has never been a corresponding cultural icon to memorialize King. While it is doubtful that the majority of persons sporting the "X" logo are drawn to the ascetic lifestyle and religious commitment that Shabazz embodied as a Muslim minister, it seems that they readily connect with the mystique of a man who made such a dramatic transition from a life of poverty and crime to become a great moral, religious, and cultural leader.

Several aspects of Shabazz's leadership style and approach are more attractive than Martin King's in light of a concern for the remoralizing task, not least of which is his own testimony of personal transformation from a demoralized state under the power of religious faith within a structured religious community. His own journey was not one from poverty to affluence but rather from demoralization to remoralization. Thus his appeal became especially credible to "the least of these" with whom he identified, and his sense of calling to reach and teach them took on special urgency and intensity, because he had been where they were. While King certainly gave attention to the disinherited in his thought and work, he seemed committed to helping them primarily by convincing and coercing whites to change their racist practices and hateful attitudes. Because of the intensity and effectiveness of his outreach to poor black males in particular, Shabazz provides a more convincing incarnation of the transformed, remoralized black male than King does. Moreover, it is with the strategy that Christians would call "evangelism" that Shabazz ministered to the disinherited—clearly, he was trying to save the souls, bodies, and spirits of an entire people. By contrast, King distanced himself from black evangelical expressions of Christianity as he embraced the concepts and worldview of white liberal theology. He retained, however, to great effect, the cadences and canons of the black preaching tradition in his communications with ecumenical, interracial audiences.

The point here is not to show that one is right and the other is wrong. Instead, the question here is to ask which approach holds more promise for creating community among African Americans, especially males, who do not share the same levels of access to educational, economic, and political opportunity. It seems evident that if African American Christian males are going to build community with men who resemble Rodney King more than Martin King, then they are going to have to develop paradigms that emphasize testimony, outreach, and spiritual nurture rather than speeches, marches, and political rhetoric. Shabazz's role was to convince black people to love themselves and to love God, and it would seem that this is a viable starting point for ethical discourse and action within the African American churches who are positioned to seek and stimulate dialogue with other racial and religious groups engaged in the quest for the beloved community. If modern Christians are unwilling to return to the "old time religion," let them at least invite attention to the paradigm of finding salvation, that is, to affirm, embody, teach, and preach the experience expressed in the words of one of the most popular songs that the African American religious tradition has borrowed from nineteenth-century European hymnody:

I once was lost, but now I'm found,
Was blind, but now I see.

This song's opening lyrics, "Amazing grace, how sweet the sound, that saved a wretch like me," were recited in a political victory speech by Marion Barry after he won reelection to the office of mayor of Washington, D. C. in November of 1994. The resurgent Barry can be viewed ostensibly as another example of a remoralized African American male engaged in the task of rebuilding community. In the winter of 1991 he was entrapped by federal law enforcement officers and videotaped while smoking crack in the hotel room of his female friend Rasheeda Moore. Subsequently, Barry was tried, convicted, and imprisoned for six months. In 1992, he won a seat on the City Council representing the poorest ward in the city. In 1994 he employed his extensive skills as a grassroots organizer to recruit volunteers, register new voters, and pull off a stunning victory over the hapless incumbent Mayor Sharon Pratt Kelly and the perennial "establishment" candidate, City Councilman John Ray. Barry attracted many votes from the black middle class, and even outpolled Mayor Kelly in her own ward. His campaign theme was revival and redemption; his campaign theme song was "I Believe," a pop release recorded by the gospel group Sounds of Blackness. He claimed that his experience of rehabilitation and incarceration had made him a better person and a more effective leader.

Marion Barry represents a compelling case study for exploration of the remoralization idea by virtue of his identification with the two Kings: He was a close associate of Martin King and was a leader in the struggle for human rights during the 1960s, but he is linked to the Rodney Kings of this world as a participant in criminal drug use and as a black male victimized by the criminal justice system and the news media. As mayor of the nation's capital, Barry was granted a renewed opportunity to encourage further political empowerment, economic development, and moral agency among the masses of people in the projects, prisons, and homeless shelters who bought into his symbolism and supported his candidacy. If history, however, judges that Barry ascended to the position of mayor only to resume the same legacy of corruption, public deception, and "charismatic" mismanagement of resources that characterized his first twelve years in office, then the image of thousands of demoralized black men and women of all economic classes finding their political voice at the polling places may ultimately be remembered as yet another illustration of intragroup victimization and exploitation.

To be effective, the proposed remoralization process has to have an evangelistic strategy and a "lost-found" paradigm based upon a tandem principle of personal and social transformation. The challenge is to identify and nurture a new generation of morally empowered African American male leaders who can demonstrate to others that power is available to restore African American males to a morally sound condition, to strengthen them in spirit, courage, discipline, and staying power, to enable them to solve their problems through restoration of mental clarity, and to bring order to the chaos of their lives. This is not exclusively the work of men, but if there is going to be any real possibility for ensuring the survival and wholeness of entire people, male and female, as womanist ethics would require, then men are going to have to play a special role in leading the whole community toward reconciliation because men have contributed mightily toward its brokenness and alienation.

Ministry

This volume was introduced with a brief critique of black liberation theology based upon the inadequacy of its ethics for those in transition from victimization to moral agency, its lack of an ethics for blacks who are "in charge" of their own institutions and resources, and its insufficient articulation and embodiment of a rationale for ongoing engagement between affluent and poor blacks. As a response, an empowerment ethics for a liberated people has been set forth in terms of six specific expressions of the moral and spiritual endeavors of African American Christians—testimony, protest, uplift, cooperation, achievement, and remoralization. The intention has been to build upon the liberation theologian's critical analysis of oppression in order to devote more attention to the moral imperatives that liberation presses upon those who are already experiencing empowerment, that is, to construct an ethics for people "in charge" of their own resources and institutions. A major concern has been the recovery of a Christian ethic that provides a rationale for empowered African American Christians and churches to remain engaged with the poor in worship and other activities that constitute ministry. In this final chapter ministry will be treated as a seventh category

that builds on the other six to round out the empowerment ethics paradigm.

The Ministry of Empowerment

Ministry is commonly understood as the professional work of
clergy who serve the needs of the church by preaching, teaching,
counseling, leading worship, and church administration. In the
African American churches, certain individuals become qualified
for ordination or licensing to do ministry in this sense generally
by acknowledging a sense of call and by undergoing some combination of mentoring and disciplined study in Bible colleges,
church institutes, or theological schools. The historical prominence of these churches as institutions of prophetic engagement
and communal empowerment is largely the fruit of efforts undertaken by African American ministers and their parishioners to ex-
tend the realm of ministry "beyond the four walls of the church"
to include response to the social problems of the people. The
field of black church studies has focused almost exclusively on the
ministry of the black preacher as church and community leader.[1]
Much has been written about individual ministers whose contributions are distinguished by their oratory and activism, and Martin Luther King, Jr., the only African American in this country
ever to be memorialized with a national holiday, was, of course, a
black preacher.

A somewhat different concept of ministry is revealed in this
survey of empowerment ethics in the thought and work of African American Christians. Both clergy and laypersons have been
named as contributors to the moral progress of African American people. Moreover, the leadership and participation of women
and the poor have been highlighted as these groups have been
empowered and have sought to empower others in the name of
Christ. This emphasis is important in view of the fact that although women constitute the vast majority of black church worshipers, and black churches are found in abundance in poor com-

munities, little attention is given in scholarly black church studies to the contributions of women and the inclusion of the poor.

Evelyn Brooks Higginbotham's *Righteous Discontent* and Albert Raboteau's *Slave Religion* are exceptional in this regard. Higginbotham argues that women empowered the church by "broadening the public arm of the church and making it the most powerful institution of racial self-help in the African American community."[2] Raboteau cites and interprets documents that give voice to the quintessential poor, that is, the slaves, "who were not silent about their religious faith" and "left their testimony as a legacy for their children and for any who wish to understand it."[3] Their testimony gave visibility and viability to the so-called invisible institution, a term ascribed by historians to the southern black churches of the slavery era. In the present study, the discussion of empowerment ethics has been heavily weighted toward the testimony of the ex-slaves and the work of black church women, because these groups provide the most impressive evidence of the vitality of the Christian gospel on the margins of the society. Ministry, therefore, is not understood here as a vehicle that merely confers professional status or certifies oratorical skill; rather, it is the meaningful progress toward human wholeness that occurs when men and women emulate Christ and undertake his mission of bringing the reign of God to bear upon all aspects of human existence.

African American liberation theologians have offered various interpretive analyses of the meaning of empowerment within the context of ministry. For example, James H. Evans, Jr., author of *We Have Been Believers: An African-American Systematic Theology*, situates spiritual empowerment within the broader agenda of liberation: "*Spiritual empowerment* is that dimension of the liberation struggle in which African-Americans come to understand and reclaim their intrinsic worth as human beings."[4] Theodore Walker, Jr., whose social ethics text *Empower the People* bears the imprint of black liberation theology, views empowerment as inclusive of emancipation, voting rights and civil rights, and the struggle for comprehensive social-economic-political and religious empowerment. He sees the struggle for comprehensive social empowerment as "essential to any quest for right relationship to God," and equates liberation and empowerment with ministry in an interesting formulation, where "service to the struggle for freedom and empowerment counts as service to God, and failure to serve this cause counts as failure to serve God."[5]

In her book *Black Feminist Thought*, Patricia Hill Collins discusses empowerment in terms of a black feminism that emphasizes resistance to black women's dehumanization on the one hand, and affirms their full humanity on the other:

> Empowerment involves rejecting the dimensions of knowledge, whether personal, cultural, or institutional, that perpetuate objectification and dehumanization. African-American women and other individuals in subordinate groups become empowered when we understand and use those dimensions of our individual, group, and disciplinary ways of knowing that foster our humanity as fully human subjects.[6]

She acknowledges the importance of personal and collective empowerment in the black woman's struggle for social change: "while individual empowerment is key, only collective action can effectively generate lasting social transformation of political and economic institutions."[7] In setting forth her Afrocentric feminist epistemology, Collins makes reference to the black church tradition and employs conceptual language and illustrations related to the ministry of the black church.[8] Within this rubric she develops two ethical constructs that underscore the connection between personal and collective empowerment, the ethic of personal accountability and the ethic of caring, which includes the capacity for empathy.[9]

The Principle of Empathy

Empathy, stated in simplest terms, is intellectual identification of oneself with another.[10] As a moral virtue, empathy involves "putting oneself in the place of the other, understanding and sharing the other's emotional experience, and seeing the world as he or she sees it."[11] From the outset, empowerment ethics has been defined in terms of the norms, principles, and ethos ascribed to individuals and groups engaged in the task of liberating others by empowering them to act. Specific examples of this ethics and ethos have been presented in view of the moral progress of African American Christians. But empathy gives special force and meaning to the ethics of empowerment in the sense that it tempers the peculiar tendency of empowered persons to divest themselves of concern for less empowered others under conditions of oppression. In other words, empathy can become an effective antidote to racism, sexism, elitism, and other forms of contempt based upon difference.

For Christians, the principle of empathy is embedded within the moral reciprocity of the Golden Rule, Jesus' admonition to treat others as you would like to be treated if you, in a way of speaking, had to trade places with them. For those African American Christians whose empowerment has come through one or more of these approaches—testimony, protest, uplift, cooperation, achievement, remoralization—the resolve to uphold the moral and social importance of identity with the dispossessed is constantly put to the test in a dominant culture where empathy is readily discarded as an impediment to the pursuit of affluence and the preservation of privilege. Empathy has given shape and direction to the ministerial formation of African American Christians across the barriers of sex and class. It provides an important key to understanding ministry as empowerment ethics.

Ministry both motivates and embodies empowerment. It is a manifestation of empowerment as spiritual formation for service. To be sure, the task of empowering others is itself a ministry, for ministry empowers those whose needs are being served. Throughout this book, inquiry has been made into the moral and spiritual meaning of various ministries of empowerment. A special effort has been made to discover which ethical imperatives have guided the thinking of liberated and empowered African American Christians engaged in various forms of ministry. It seems appropriate, therefore, to conclude with a summary analysis of the interplay between empathy and empowerment in ministry, as observed within the various stages of moral and spiritual progress described in the preceding chapters with reference to African American Christianity. Such an approach will, we hope, contribute to an increased appreciation of the ethical complexity of ministerial formation as it has occurred among African American Christians, many of whom have followed Jesus with the understanding that his conception of his mission, as H. Richard Niebuhr once asserted, "can never be forced into the pattern of an emancipator from merely human oppressions."[12]

An African American Christian Witness: Empowering the People

In view of the present critical need to designate an ethics of empowerment for African American Christians who are (1) already experiencing liberation, (2) in charge of their own resources and institutions, and (3) inclined to disengage themselves from the concerns and company of the poor, several lessons can be learned from the thought and experience of those who have sought to empower their own people by means of such avenues as testimony, protest, uplift, cooperation among the sexes, achievement in education and the professions, and the dynamics of remoralization.

The testimony of the experience of *conversion* to Christianity signified an important locus of personal and collective spiritual empowerment for the otherwise dispossessed African American slave. The high value ascribed to expressions of empathy within the slave community led to adoption of a variety of ethical styles in confronting the evil of slavery. Lying to and stealing from whites were justified under the conditions of oppression for those slaves who adhered to a situation ethics. Their ethic of justice, however, empowered them to respond morally to adverse social conditions with a critique of the hypocrisy of their white Christian oppressors, whom they regarded as slaveholding liars and thieves. The slaves knew better than to emulate the bogus morality of their oppressors. It seems that their moral empowerment entailed the ability to maintain some meaningful sense of morality and justice that transcends the ethos of oppression, no matter how attractively articulated or impressively documented it appeared. As theodicy, slave testimony revealed deep reflection upon the purpose of freedom and human suffering from the vantage point of total familiarity with the slave past and uncertainty about what emancipation would bring. In the course of making the transition from slavery to freedom, the ex-slave Christians struggled to be faithful to God's call to freedom and justice in a society that offered attractive compromises with the evils of oppression. The testimony of conversion enabled them to share the empowerment they experienced as divine affirmation of their own humanity and as prayerful participation in the pursuit of freedom and justice within the worshiping community.

Protest can be a vicarious form of political empowerment, a ministry of social activism conducted by individuals and groups who voice the complaints of the oppressed. David Walker and Maria Steward were free black Christian abolitionists in the North whose empathy on behalf of the slaves in the South found expression in their speeches and writings. Walker held whites and blacks equally accountable to the Golden Rule. He challenged whites to end slavery based upon a Christian obligation to treat blacks as they themselves wanted to be treated, and called for blacks to exercise their responsibility to emancipate, educate, and evangelize not only themselves but also other oppressed peoples all over the world. He promoted a peculiar form of empathy that would require blacks to use violent means to secure their freedom, insofar as the Golden Rule obligates them to protect and defend themselves from mistreatment. Maria Steward enumerated the sins of white America—slavery, murder, and the sexual subjugation of black slave women. She encouraged black women to see their families, schools, and businesses as spheres of educational and economic empowerment. While Steward refrained from recommending violent means to force resolution of black demands, she insisted that prayers for deliverance and human rights claims be supplemented with self-help ethics and moral improvement. Another form of protest is the spoken and written advocacy of modern black intellectuals on behalf of poor urban blacks. Glenn Loury and Cornel West, respectively, offer conservative and liberal critical analyses of the prospects for black moral progress from the intellectual vantage point of empathy for and advocacy on behalf of the oppressed. In their scholarly zeal to critique each other, however, both have abandoned the scriptural and theological bases that empowered the empathetic discourse of protest articulated by the two nineteenth-century abolitionists.

The *uplift* efforts of the black women's clubs and church groups carried forward the agenda begun in the aftermath of slavery, namely, to educate, evangelize, and improve the economic and social environment of poor blacks. Clearly, empathy is the pretext of the theme "lifting as we climb." Ethicist Marcia Riggs formulates their approach to ministry in empathy with the poor and ignorant masses of blacks in terms of three concepts: renunciation, inclusivity, and responsibility. She commends the moral vision of the black club women to modern-day liberationists as a guide to the ongoing socioeconomic praxis of black liberation. Two black women leaders in the ministry of uplift, Nannie Helen Burroughs and Mary McLeod Bethune, expressed their empathy with the plight of poor blacks in public speeches and via the establishment of educational institutions designed to promote the social empowerment of black youth. The ministry of uplift was also emphasized by the Holiness churches, who sought the social and ecclesial empowerment of women and the poor for theological reasons.

Three empowering models of male-female *cooperation* have been unearthed from the early history of the Holiness-

Pentecostal tradition in the United States: egalitarian, charismatic, and dialectical. The egalitarian cooperation of the sexes that characterized the origins of the predominantly black National Association of the Church of God ultimately clarified their resolve to reject the racist practices of whites in the same religious body, and to encourage interracial openness grounded in a strong antiracist posture of empathy. The apostle of the Azusa Street Revival, William J. Seymour, promoted the charismatic leadership and participation of women, but became profoundly disillusioned by the racism of white tongues-speaking Christians, both male and female, who undermined his efforts to expand the interracial outreach of the Revival. The dialectics of protest and cooperation was developed by women in the Church of God in Christ in order to enable the exercise of their charismatic gifts in a male-dominated denomination. They exhibited a peculiar form of empathy with the men in response to the racism of the larger society, at one point committing themselves to hold the church "together and in harness" until the men were able to resume leadership of the denomination after the death of its founder, Bishop C. H. Mason. Each of these three models of male-female cooperation represents a distinctive approach to the empowerment of black women for ministry. On the whole, the emergent Holiness-Pentecostal movement influenced the historical evolution of religion in the United States by cultivating empathetic engagement with blacks, women, and the poor at all levels of ministry.

The *achievement* of middle-class status through education and professional employment remains one of the most palpable forms of black economic empowerment. Special attention has been given to the educational and professional advancement of black women, notwithstanding their lack of access to the upper echelons of white and black corporate management. In this context, the empathy of professional black women is often expressed as a sense of personal and collective guilt over the unrealized social role of the black middle class in relation to the black poor. Indeed, the convergence of womanist and Christian ethics in the church and community involvement of professional black women underscores the imperative to empathize with the predicament of the black family, and to provide meaningful role models for black youth. In this perspective, the ministry of empowerment is not merely intended to inspire black youth to acquire middle-class status by means of education and professional employment as an end in itself; instead, the goal is to invite them to share in the task of providing abundant life for all persons.

Remoralization is offered as a descriptive term for several approaches to reversing the effects of demoralization among black people generally, and especially among black males, toward the end of empowerment for personal and social change. The social ethical dilemma of African Americans is illumined by the story of two Kings, Martin and Rodney, whose victimization evoked violent conflagrations in America's cities. Martin King has captured the attention of an entire generation of black male theologians and ethicists who have generally failed to address important intragroup ethical concerns. Rodney King's brutal beating by Los Angeles police officers elicited a host of expressions of outrage, but little has been said about his persistent pattern of antisocial behavior. The prospects for effecting a reconciliation between the men who think like Martin King and those who behave like Rodney King are largely dependent upon the willingness of middle-class black Christians to empathize with demoralized black males. El-Hajj Malik El-Shabazz (Malcolm X) is lifted up as a significant symbol of remoralization and empathy in the context of the Islamic faith; his experience of spiritual transformation caused him to abandon a life of crime and to engage in an effective ministry of outreach and empowerment among the masses of urban blacks. This example is cited as a challenge to African American Christians to revisit the imperative to evangelize the "lost" by promoting empowerment and empathy in community-building ministries.

The willingness of African American Christians to retain an open moral and spiritual commitment to empathy may prove to be the key to this nation's ability to marshal its moral and fiscal resources to liberate the poor within its own borders. The ethics of empowerment challenges religious leaders to embody creative approaches to personal growth and collective resourcefulness for meeting human need, and to resist the temptation to follow the path of "cheap justice" that demands repentance and restitution from the oppressing group on behalf of the poor without engaging in a self-critical assessment of the full cost of the equitable sharing of one's own power and resources. It is hoped that increasing numbers of religious and moral leaders will step forward who are willing to prod themselves toward cultivating character-producing structures that embody the noblest ethical ideals being preached and taught in the name of Christ. The distinctive calling of the African American Christian community at the close of the twentieth century is full implementation of the ethics of empowerment, so that the disinherited can be motivated to hope, and the privileged can be challenged to do justice.

Notes

Introduction. *Ethics for a People in Charge*

1. Among books by contemporary African American ethicists writing in the black liberation tradition are: Garth Baker-Fletcher, *Somebodyness: Martin Luther King, Jr. and the Theory of Dignity*, Harvard Dissertations in Religion (Minneapolis: Fortress Press, 1993); Lewis V. Baldwin, *To Make the Wounded Whole: The Cultural Legacy of Martin Luther King, Jr.* (Minneapolis: Fortress Press, 1992); Katie G. Cannon, *Black Womanist Ethics* (Atlanta: Scholars Press, 1988); Riggins R. Earl, Jr., *Dark Symbols, Obscure Signs: God, Self, and Community in the Slave Mind*, rev. ed. (Maryknoll, N.Y.: Orbis Books, 1993); Robert M. Franklin, *Liberating Visions: Human Fulfillment and Social Justice in African-American Thought* (Minneapolis: Fortress Press, 1990); Walter E. Fluker, *They Looked for a City: A Comparative Analysis of the Ideal of Community in the Thought of Howard Thurman and Martin Luther King, Jr.* (Lanham, Md.: University Press of America, 1989); Enoch H. Oglesby, *Born in the Fire: Case Studies in Christian Ethics and Globalization* (Cleveland: Pilgrim Press, 1990); Peter J. Paris, *The Social Teaching of the Black Churches* (Philadelphia: Fortress Press, 1985); Marcia Y. Riggs, *Awake, Arise and Act: A Womanist Call for Black Liberation* (Cleveland: Pilgrim Press, 1994); Emilie M. Townes, *Womanist Justice, Womanist Hope* (Atlanta: Scholars Press, 1993); Darryl M. Trimiew, *Voices of the Silenced: The Responsible Self in a Marginalized Community* (St. Louis: Chalice Press, 1994); and Theodore Walker, Jr., *Empower the People: Social Ethics for the African American Church* (Maryknoll, N.Y.: Orbis Books, 1991).

2. C. Eric Lincoln and Lawrence H. Mamiya, *The Black Church in the African American Experience* (Durham, N.C.: Duke University Press, 1990), 179.

3. See Dietrich Bonhoeffer, *The Cost of Discipleship*, trans. R. H. Fuller (New York: Macmillan, 1948).

Chapter 1. *Testimony*

1. William L. Andrews, introduction to *Sisters of the Spirit: Three Black Women's Autobiographies of the Nineteenth Century*, ed. William L. Andrews (Bloomington: Indiana University Press, 1986), 1.

2. George P. Rawick, ed., *The American Slave: A Composite Autobiography*, 19 vols. (Westport, Conn.: Greenwood Press, 1972, 1977). See also Clifton H. Johnson, ed., *God Struck Me Dead: Voices of Ex-Slaves* (Cleveland: Pilgrim Press, 1993).

3. For detailed discussion of the diverse social ethical views of ex-slaves, see Cheryl J. Sanders, *Slavery and Conversion: An Analysis of Ex-Slave Testimony* (Th.D. thesis, Harvard University, 1985), and "Liberation Ethics in the Ex-Slave Interviews," in *Cut Loose Your Stammering Tongue: Black Theology in the Slave Narratives*, Dwight Hopkins and George Cummings, eds. (Maryknoll, N.Y.: Orbis Books, 1991).

4. Thomas W. Ogletree, *The Use of the Bible in Christian Ethics* (Philadelphia: Fortress Press, 1983), 187.

5. Mary Reynolds, in Rawick, *The American Slave*, Vol. 5, Pt. 3, 246.

6. Booker T. Washington, *Up from Slavery* in *Three Negro Classics* (New York: Avon Books, 1965), 31.

7. Quoted in Albert J. Raboteau, *Slave Religion: The Invisible Institution in the Antebellum South* (New York: Oxford University Press, 1978), 296.

8. Ibid.

9. Ibid., 295.

10. Ibid.

11. Quoted by Olli Alho, *The Religion of the Slaves* (Helsinki: Academia Scientarium Fennica, 1976), 188.

12. Raboteau, *Slave Religion*, 296.

13. Ibid.

14. Ibid.

15. Alho, *The Religion of the Slaves*, 188.

16. Paul D. Escott, *Slavery Remembered: Record of Twentieth-Century Slave Narratives* (Chapel Hill: University of North Carolina Press, 1979), 115.

17. Ibid., 113–14.

18. Raboteau, *Slave Religion*, 291–92.

19. Escott, *Slavery Remembered*, 114.

20. Raboteau, *Slave Religion*, 309.

21. Ibid., 310.

22. Ibid., 314.

23. Miss Catherine, in Rawick, *The American Slave*, Vol. 18, 210.

24. Mary Ellen Johnson, in Rawick, Suppl. Ser. 2, Vol. 6, Pt. 5, 2032–33.

25. Virginia Harris, in Rawick, Suppl. Ser. 1, Vol. 8, Pt. 3, 946.

26. Hannah Davidson, in Rawick, Vol. 16, 26ff.

27. David Brion Davis, *Slavery and Human Progress* (New York: Oxford University Press, 1984), 16.

28. Ellen Payne, in Rawick, *The American Slave,* Suppl. Ser. 2, Vol. 8, Pt. 7, 3043.

29. Lucy, in Rawick, Vol. 18, 24–25.

30. Anderson Edwards, in Rawick, Suppl. Ser. 2, Vol. 4, Pt. 3, 1268.

Chapter 2. *Protest*

1. David Walker, *David Walker's Appeal,* Charles M. Wiltse, ed. (New York: Hill and Wang, 1965); Maria M. Steward, "Religion and the Pure Principles of Morality," in *Early Negro Writing, 1760–1837,* Dorothy Porter, ed. (Boston: Beacon Press, 1971).

2. The source of this biographical information on Walker is Wiltse's "Introduction" to *David Walker's Appeal,* vii–xii.

3. *David Walker's Appeal,* 70.

4. Ibid., 29–30.

5. Ibid., 75.

6. The source of this biographical information on Steward is *Black Women in White America: A Documentary History,* Gerda Lerner, ed. (New York: Vintage Books, 1972), 83–84.

7. Maria W. Steward, "Religion and the Pure Principles of Morality," 465–66.

8. Ibid., 469.

9. Ibid., 470.

10. Ibid., 466.

11. Ibid., 468.

12. Ibid., 461.

13. Ibid., 470–71.

14. See Garth Baker-Fletcher, *Somebodyness: Martin Luther King, Jr., and the Theory of Dignity,* Harvard Dissertations in Religion (Minneapolis: Fortress Press, 1993) and "King's Late View of Dignity, 1962–1968: Seven Motivic Concepts," *Journal of Religious Thought* 48, no. 2 (Winter-Spring 1991–1992):18–31; Lewis V. Baldwin, *There Is a Balm in Gilead: The Cultural Roots of Martin Luther King, Jr.* (Minneapolis: Fortress Press, 1990) and *To Make the Wounded Whole: The Cultural Legacy of Martin Luther King, Jr.* (Minneapolis: Fortress Press, 1992); James H. Cone, *Martin & Malcolm & America: A Dream or a Nightmare* (Maryknoll, N.Y.: Orbis Books, 1991); Noel Leo Erskine, *King among the Theologians* (Cleveland: Pilgrim Press, 1994) and "King and the Black Church," *Journal of Religious Thought* 48, no. 2 (Winter-Spring 1991–1992):9–15; Robert M. Franklin, *Liberating Visions: Human Fulfillment and Social Justice in African-American Thought* (Minneapolis: Fortress Press,

1990) and "In Pursuit of a Just Society: Martin Luther King, Jr., and John Rawls," *Journal of Religious Ethics* 18, no. 2 (Fall 1990):57–77; Walter Fluker, *They Looked for a City: A Comparative Analysis of the Ideal of Community in the Thought of Howard Thurman and Martin Luther King, Jr.* (Lanham, Md.: University Press of America, 1989) and "They Looked for a City: A Comparison of the Ideal of Community in Howard Thurman and Martin Luther King, Jr.," *Journal of Religious Ethics* 18, no. 2 (Fall 1990):33–55; Peter J. Paris, *Black Religious Leaders: Conflict in Unity* (Louisville: Westminster/John Knox Press, 1991); Cornel West, "Martin Luther King, Jr.: Prophetic Christian as Organic Intellectual," and "The Prophetic Tradition in Afro-America," in *Prophetic Fragments* (reprint; Grand Rapids, Mich.: Wm. B. Eerdmans, 1993); and Preston N. Williams, "An Analysis of the Conception of Love and Its Influence on Justice in the Thought of Martin Luther King, Jr.," *Journal of Religious Ethics* 18, no. 2 (Fall 1990):15–32.

15. Glenn C. Loury, "A Prescription for Black Progress," *The Christian Century* (April 30, 1986), 434.

16. Loury, "The Moral Quandary of the Black Community," *The Public Interest,* No. 79 (Spring 1985), 11.

17. Ibid.

18. Cornel West, "Unmasking the Black Conservatives," *The Christian Century* (July 16–23, 1986), 646.

19. Ibid., 644.

20. Ibid., 646.

21. Ibid.

22. West, *Race Matters* (Boston: Beacon Press, 1993), 11.

23. Ibid.

24. Ibid., 12.

25. Ibid., 19–20.

26. West, "Martin Luther King, Jr.," 3.

Chapter 3. *Uplift*

1. Paula Giddings, *When and Where I Enter: The Impact of Black Women on Race and Sex in America* (New York: William Morrow, 1984), 98.

2. Ibid.

3. Ibid., 97.

4. For ethical and theological studies of the black women's clubs see also Karen Baker-Fletcher's *A Singing Something: Womanist Reflections on Anna Julia Cooper* (New York: Crossroad, 1994), and two books by Emilie M. Townes: *Womanist Justice, Womanist Hope* (Atlanta: Scholars Press, 1993) and *In a Blaze of Glory: Womanist Spirituality as Social Witness* (Nashville: Abingdon Press, 1995).

5. Marcia Y. Riggs, *Awake, Arise and Act: A Womanist Call for Black Liberation* (Cleveland: Pilgrim Press, 1994), 97.

6. Ibid., 95.

7. Evelyn Brooks Higginbotham, *Righteous Discontent: The Women's Movement in the Black Baptist Church, 1880–1920* (Cambridge: Harvard University Press, 1993), 1–2.

8. Ibid., 187.

9. Ibid., 228.

10. Theodore Walker, Jr., *Empower the People: Social Ethics for the African American Church* (Maryknoll, N.Y.: Orbis Books, 1991), 108.

11. Higginbotham, *Righteous Discontent*, 228–29.

12. Ibid., 228.

13. In a conversation with the author, the Reverend James Scott of Baltimore, Maryland, now deceased, shared his remembrances of the great preaching ability of Miss Burroughs as she made numerous appearances in the Baltimore churches.

14. Nannie H. Burroughs, "Unload Your Uncle Toms," in *Black Women in White America: A Documentary History*, Gerda Lerner, ed. (New York: Vintage Books, 1972), 551–53.

15. Nannie H. Burroughs, "Who Started Woman's Day?" in *Women and Religion in America: 1900–1986*, Vol. 3, Rosemary Radford Ruether and Rosemary Skinner Keller, eds. (New York: Harper and Row, 1986), 124.

16. Ibid., 125.

17. Evelyn Brooks Barnett, "Nannie Burroughs and the Education of Black Women," in *The Afro-American Woman: Struggles and Images*, Sharon Harley and Rosalyn Terborg-Penn, eds. (Port Washington, N.Y.: Kennikat Press, 1978), 107–08.

18. Giddings, *When and Where I Enter*, 199.

19. Ibid., 229–30.

20. Ibid., 228.

21. Clarence G. Newsome, "Mary McLeod Bethune as Religionist," in *Women in New Worlds*, Vol. 1, Hilah F. Thomas and Rosemary Skinner Keller, eds. (Nashville: Abingdon, 1981), 115–16.

22. Excerpted from Mary McLeod Bethune, "My Last Will and Testament," in Ruether and Keller, *Women and Religion in America*, 3:97–99.

23. Nancy Hardesty, Lucille Sider Dayton, Donald W. Dayton, "Women in the Holiness Movement: Feminism in the Evangelical Tradition," in *Women of Spirit*, Rosemary Radford Ruether and Eleanor McLaughlin, eds. (New York: Simon and Schuster, 1979), 233.

24. Susie Stanley, "Women Evangelists in the Church of God at the Beginning of the Twentieth Century," in *Called to Minister, Empowered to Serve*, Juanita Leonard, ed. (Anderson, Ind.: Warner Press, 1989), 41.

25. Ruth A. Tucker and Walter L. Liefeld, *Daughters of the Church: Women and Ministry from New Testament Times to the Present* (Grand Rapids: Academie Books, 1987), 262.

26. Stanley, "Women Evangelists," 50–53.

27. Hardesty, Dayton, and Dayton, "Women in the Holiness Movement," 238–39.

28. Tucker and Liefeld, *Daughters of the Church,* 371.

29. Ibid., 264–67.

30. Norris Magnuson, *Salvation in the Slums: Evangelical Social Work, 1865–1920* (Metuchen, N.J.: Scarecrow Press, 1977), 41.

31. Ibid., xvi.

32. Ibid., 165–66.

33. William J. Seymour, quoted by Iain MacRobert, *The Black Roots and White Racism of Early Pentecostalism in the U.S.A.* (London: MacMillan Press, 1988), 48.

34. Jualyne E. Dodson and Cheryl Townsend Gilkes, "Something Within: Social Change and Collective Endurance in the Sacred World of Black Christian Women," in Ruether and Keller, *Women and Religion in America,* 3:87.

35. Robert Mapes Anderson, *Vision of the Disinherited: The Making of American Pentecostalism* (New York: Oxford University Press, 1979), 151–52.

36. Jerry G. Watts, "Class, Race and Poverty USA," in *Christianity and Crisis* (May 16, 1988), 186.

Chapter 4. *Cooperation*

1. For critical discussion of sexism in the black churches, see Kelly Brown Douglas, *The Black Christ* (Maryknoll, N.Y.: Orbis Books, 1994); Cain Hope Felder, *Troubling Biblical Waters: Race, Class, and Family* (Maryknoll, N.Y.: Orbis Books, 1989); Ella P. Mitchell, ed., *Women: To Preach or Not to Preach* (Valley Forge, Pa.: Judson Press, 1992); and Delores S. Williams, *Sisters in the Wilderness: The Challenge of Womanist God-Talk* (Maryknoll, N.Y.: Orbis Books, 1993). Clarice Martin's "The *Haustafeln* (Household Codes) in African American Biblical Interpretation: 'Free Slaves' and Subordinate Women," in *Stony the Road We Trod: African American Biblical Interpretation,* Cain Hope Felder, ed. (Minneapolis: Fortress Press, 1991), provides an insightful treatment of the biblical hermeneutics and sexist practices in these churches.

2. Roger Finke and Rodney Stark, *The Churching of America, 1776–1990: Winners and Losers in Our Religious Economy* (New Brunswick: Rutgers University Press, 1992), 5.

3. Ibid., 237.

4. Donald W. Dayton, "Yet Another Layer of the Onion, Or Opening the Ecumenical Door to Let the Riffraff In," *The Ecumenical Review* 40, no. 1 (January 1988): 93.

5. Ibid., 108.

6. Cheryl Townsend Gilkes, "The Role of Women in the Sanctified Church," *Journal of Religious Thought* 43, no. 1 (Spring-Summer 1986): 34.

7. Dayton, "Yet Another Layer of the Onion," 106.

8. Susie Cunningham Stanley, quoted by Timothy C. Morgan, "The Stained-Glass Ceiling," *Christianity Today* (May 16, 1994), 52.

9. Susie Cunningham Stanley, *Feminist Pillar of Fire: The Life of Alma White* (Cleveland: Pilgrim Press, 1993), 2.

10. Morgan, "The Stained-Glass Ceiling," 52.

11. Charles E. Brown, "Women Preachers," *The Gospel Trumpet* (May 27, 1939), 5.

12. William C. Turner, Jr., "Movements in the Spirit: A Review of African American Holiness/Pentecostal/Apostolics," in *Directory of African American Religious Bodies*, Wardell Payne, ed. (Washington, D.C.: Howard University Press, 1991), 248.

13. Statistics cited in *1995 Yearbook of the Church of God* (Anderson, Ind.: Leadership Council of the Church of God, 1995), 337, and *Commemorative Booklet in Observance of the Centennial Celebration of the Church of God, 1880–1980* (West Middlesex, Pa.: National Association of the Church of God, 1981), 87.

14. Katie H. Davis, ed., *Zion's Hill at West Middlesex* (Anderson, Ind.: Shining Light Press, 1985), 10–11.

15. Ibid., 27.

16. Ibid., 28.

17. Ibid., 11.

18. Ibid., 24.

19. Ibid., 19.

20. Ibid., 12.

21. Ibid., 29–30.

22. Samuel G. Hines, with Joe Allison, *Experience the Power* (Anderson, Ind.: Warner Press, 1993), 91.

23. Davis, *Zion's Hill*, 47.

24. Ibid.

25. This account of Seymour's role in the Azusa Street Revival is adapted from several sources. See Joseph Colletti, "Selected Historical Pentecostal Sites in the Los Angeles Area" (Pasadena, Calif.: David J. du Plessis Center for Christian Spirituality); Leonard Lovett, "Aspects of the Spiritual Legacy of the Church of God in Christ: Ecumenical Implications," in *Black Witness to the Apostolic Faith,* David T. Shannon and Gayraud S. Wilmore, eds. (Grand Rapids: Wm. B. Eerdmans, 1985, 1988); Cecil M. Robeck, Jr., "Azusa Street Revival" and "Bonnie Brae Street Cottage," and H. Vinson Synan, "William Joseph Seymour," in *Dictionary of Pentecostal and Charismatic Movements,* Stanley M. Burgess and Gary B. McGee, eds. (Grand Rapids: Zondervan, 1988); and James S. Tinney, "William J. Seymour: Father of Modern-Day Pentecostalism," in *Black Apostles: Afro-American Clergy Confront the Twentieth Century,* Randall K. Burkett and Richard Newman, eds. (Boston: G. K. Hall, 1978).

26. Harvey Cox, *Fire from Heaven: Pentecostalism, Spirituality, and the Re-*

shaping of Religion in the Twenty-First Century (Reading, Mass.: Addison-Wesley, 1995), 49.

27. Ibid., xv.
28. Turner, "Movements in the Spirit," 251.
29. Ibid.
30. Cox, *Fire from Heaven*, 63.
31. Ibid., 64.
32. Synan, "William Joseph Seymour," 781.
33. Robeck, "Asuza Street Revival," 35.
34. Cheryl Townsend Gilkes, "'Together and in Harness': Women's Traditions in the Sanctified Church," in *Black Women in America: Social Science Perspectives,* Micheline R. Malson, Elisabeth Mudimbe-Boyi, Jean F. O'Barr, and Mary Wyer, eds. (Chicago: University of Chicago Press, 1990), 229. This article was originally published in *Signs* 10, no. 4 (Summer 1985).
35. Ibid., 237.
36. Ibid.
37. Ibid., 229.
38. Ibid., 240.
39. Ibid.
40. Ibid., 225.
41. Ibid.
42. Ibid., 235.
43. Ibid., 231.
44. Ibid.
45. Ibid., 242.

Chapter 5. *Achievement*

1. Jeanne Noble, *Beautiful, Also, Are the Souls of My Black Sisters: A History of the Black Woman in America* (Englewood Cliffs: Prentice-Hall, 1978), 67–68.
2. Paula Giddings, *When and Where I Enter: The Impact of Black Women on Race and Sex in America* (New York: William Morrow, 1984), 7.
3. Noble, *Beautiful, Also, Are the Souls of My Black Sisters,* 129.
4. Jacqueline Trescott and Dorothy Gilliam, "The New Black Woman," *The Washington Post* (28–30 December 1986).
5. Ibid. (28 December 1986), A9.
6. Ibid. (29 December 1986), A7.
7. Cheryl Townsend Gilkes, "'Together and in Harness': Women's Traditions in the Sanctified Church," in *Black Women in America: Social Science Perspectives,* Micheline R. Malson, Elisabeth Mudimbe-Boyi, Jean F. O'Barr, and Mary Wyer, eds. (Chicago: University of Chicago Press, 1990), 232.
8. Ibid., 234.
9. See Clarence G. Newsome's chapter on "Mary McLeod Bethune as Reli-

gionist," in *Women in New Worlds,* Hilah F. Thomas and Rosemary Skinner Keller, eds. (Nashville: Abingdon Press, 1981) and Evelyn Brooks's article "Religion, Politics and Gender: The Leadership of Nannie Helen Burroughs," in *Journal of Religious Thought* 44, no. 2 (Winter-Spring, 1988).

10. These first publications include Katie G. Cannon, *Black Womanist Ethics* (Atlanta: Scholars Press, 1988); Toinette M. Eugene, "Moral Values and Black Womanists," *Journal of Religious Thought* 44, no. 2 (Winter-Spring 1988):23–34; Cheryl Townsend Gilkes, "The Role of Women in the Sanctified Church," *Journal of Religious Thought* 43, no. 1 (Spring-Summer 1986): 24–41; Jacquelyn Grant, "Womanist Theology," *Journal of the Interdenominational Theological Center* 13 (Spring 1986):195–212; Renita J. Weems, *Just a Sister Away: A Womanist Vision of Women's Relationships in the Bible* (San Diego: LuraMedia, 1988); and Delores S. Williams, "Womanist Theology: Black Women's Voices," *Christianity and Crisis* (July 14, 1986):230–32. See also my edited volume *Living the Intersection: Womanism and Afrocentrism in Theology* (Minneapolis: Fortress Press, 1995).

11. Alice Walker, *In Search of Our Mothers' Gardens: Womanist Prose* (New York: Harcourt Brace Jovanovich, 1983), xi–xii.

12. Trescott and Gilliam, "The New Black Woman" (28 December 1986), A8.

13. Cheryl J. Sanders et al., "Christian Ethics and Theology in Womanist Perspective," *Journal of Feminist Studies in Religion* 5, no. 2 (Fall 1989): 83–112.

14. Cheryl Townsend Gilkes, in ibid., 109.

15. Walker, *In Search of Our Mothers' Gardens,* xi–xii.

16. Katie G. Cannon, *Black Womanist Ethics,* 17.

17. See William Raspberry's editorial, "Teach Them to Praise the 'Brainiacs,'" *The Washington Post* (25 March 1987).

18. Eleanor Holmes Norton, "Restoring the Traditional Black Family," *New York Times Magazine* (2 June 1985), 96.

19. Gilkes, "'Together and in Harness,'" 232.

20. Joyce Ladner, "Washington, Save Your Children," *The Washington Post* (24 January 1988), C2.

21. Ibid.

22. George Davis and Glegg Watson, *Black Life in Corporate America: Swimming in the Mainstream* (Garden City, N.Y.: Anchor/Doubleday, 1982), 135.

23. Trescott and Gilliam, "The New Black Woman" (28 December 1986), A8.

24. Eugene, "Moral Values and Black Womanists," 35.

25. Ibid., 30.

26. Davis and Watson, *Black Life in Corporate America,* 130.

27. Preston N. Williams, "Ethics and Ethos in the Black Experience," *Christianity and Crisis* (May 31, 1971), 109.

Chapter 6. *Remoralization*

1. See Taylor Branch, *Parting the Waters: America in the King Years, 1954–63* (New York: Simon and Schuster, 1988); David J. Garrow, *Bearing the Cross: Martin Luther King, Jr. and the Southern Christian Leadership Conference* (New York: Vintage Books, 1986) and *The FBI and Martin Luther King, Jr.* (New York: Penguin Books, 1981); and Stephen Oates, *Let the Trumpet Sound: The Life of Martin Luther King, Jr.* (New York: Harper & Row, 1982).

2. Lewis V. Baldwin, *To Make the Wounded Whole: The Cultural Legacy of Martin Luther King, Jr.* (Minneapolis: Fortress Press, 1992), 301.

3. See Alice Walker's complete definition of "womanist" in the preface to *In Search of Our Mothers' Gardens: Womanist Prose* (San Diego: Harcourt Brace Jovanovich, 1983).

4. See Paula Giddings, *When and Where I Enter: The Impact of Black Women on Race and Sex in America* (New York: William Morrow, 1984), 312–14.

5. Noel Leo Erskine, *King among the Theologians* (Cleveland: Pilgrim Press, 1994), 159ff.

6. Preston N. Williams, "An Analysis of the Conception of Love and Its Influence on Justice in the Thought of Martin Luther King, Jr.," *Journal of Religious Ethics* 18, no. 2 (Fall 1990): 25, 29.

7. Katie G. Cannon, *Black Womanist Ethics* (Atlanta: Scholars Press, 1988), 174.

8. Ibid.

9. Marcia Y. Riggs, "Ethics for Living a Dream Deferred," *Drew Gateway* 59, no. 1 (Fall 1989): 14.

10. Ibid., 18.

11. From *Webster's New Universal Unabridged Dictionary*, Second Edition (Cleveland: New World Dictionary, 1983).

12. John G. Gammie, *Holiness in Israel*, Overtures to Biblical Theology (Minneapolis: Fortress Press, 1989), 195–96.

13. Ibid., 196.

14. Wilson J. Moses, "Civil Religion and the Crisis of Civil Rights," *Drew Gateway* 56, no. 1 (Winter 1986): 40–41.

15. Ibid.

16. Harold Dean Trulear, "The Black Middle Class Church and the Quest for Community," *Drew Gateway* 61, no. 1 (Fall 1991): 56.

17. Ibid., 58–59.

18. Ibid., 47–48.

19. See Malcolm X with Alex Haley, *The Autobiography of Malcolm X* (New York: Ballantine Books, 1964). He is referred to here as Shabazz and not as Malcolm X in deference to the fact that toward the end of his life he adopted the former name to signify a further stage in his own spiritual pilgrimage.

Chapter 7. *Ministry*

1. Among the most frequently cited works on the black churches are E. Franklin Frazier and C. Eric Lincoln, *The Negro Church in America* and *The Black Church Since Frazier* (New York: Schocken Books, 1974); C. Eric Lincoln and Lawrence H. Mamiya, *The Black Church in the African American Experience* (Durham, N.C.: Duke University Press, 1990); Peter J. Paris, *Black Religious Leaders: Conflict in Unity* (Louisville: Westminster/John Knox Press, 1991) and *The Social Teaching of the Black Churches* (Philadelphia: Fortress Press, 1985); Albert J. Raboteau, *Slave Religion: The Invisible Institution in the Antebellum South* (New York: Oxford University Press, 1978); Gayraud Wilmore, *Black Religion and Black Radicalism: An Interpretation of the Religious History of Afro-American People* (Garden City, N.Y.: Doubleday Anchor Books, 1972).

2. Evelyn Brooks Higginbotham, *Righteous Discontent: The Women's Movement in the Black Baptist Church* (Cambridge, Mass.: Harvard University Press, 1993), 1.

3. Raboteau, *Slave Religion*, 321.

4. James H. Evans, Jr., *We Have Been Believers: An African-American Systematic Theology* (Minneapolis: Fortress Press, 1992), 17.

5. Theodore Walker, Jr., *Empower the People: Social Ethics for the African-American Church* (Maryknoll, N.Y.: Orbis Books, 1991), 30.

6. Patricia Hill Collins, *Black Feminist Thought: Knowledge, Consciousness, and the Politics of Empowerment* (New York: Routledge, 1991), 230.

7. Ibid., 237.

8. For a critique of Collins's understanding of the black church as an arena of black female power, see Cheryl J. Sanders, "Afrocentrism and Womanism in the Seminary," *Christianity and Crisis* 52, nos. 5/6 (April 13, 1992): 126.

9. Collins, *Black Feminist Thought*, 215–19.

10. *Webster's New Universal Unabridged Dictionary*, Second Edition (Cleveland: New World Dictionaries, 1983).

11. Graeme M. Griffin, "Empathy," in *The Westminster Dictionary of Christian Ethics*, James F. Childress and John Macquarrie, eds. (Philadelphia: The Westminster Press, 1986), 190–91.

12. H. Richard Niebuhr, *Christ and Culture* (New York: Harper Colophon Books, 1951, 1975), 110.

Index

A Note on the Cover Art

JOHN BIGGERS. *Shotguns,* oil and acrylic on canvas, 1987. 40 × 56 inches. Private collection. Used by permission of the artist. Photo courtesy of the Dallas Museum of Art.

The concept of ascension, of the rising spirit, is presented in this scene of the black community in Houston's Third Ward. Women stand on porches and hold in their hands miniature houses very much like the shrines of the home. Like black caryatids that support their households, these women are for Biggers the archetypes of their community. He brings to his work his interest in African textiles. The overall patterning of the painting—rooftops of shotgun houses—is clearly derived from Kuba cloth patterns. The railroad track is itself a horizontal path of the ghetto, a symbol of migration, mechanization, and the spread of the Diaspora from the South to the North. It represents both the underground railroad and a contemporary passage to a better way of life. The Africanized features of these indomitable women who remained behind and their royal bearing are testimony to the strength of their heritage. The ascension of the birds suggests a spirituality in the community which sustains the necessary resolve for a people's continuity.

—From Alvia J. Wardlaw et al., *Black Art: Ancestral Legacy: The African Impulse in African-American Art,* ed. Robert V. Rozelle (Dallas: Dallas Museum of Art, 1989)

CPSIA information can be obtained at www.ICGtesting.com
Printed in the USA
BVOW012012050112

279926BV00001B/12/A